Barris
TV & MOVIE CARS

George Barris & David Fetherston

MBI Publishing Company

■
Dedication

This book is dedicated to all the actors, directors, producers, and cameramen with whom
I've had the pleasure of working in the film and television industry for the past forty-six years,
including the stuntmen, fabricators, gaffers, riggers, make-up folks, sound technicians, and production crew.
Thanks for all the great times, the fun, and the opportunity to be part of this marvelous business of entertaining people.

First published in 1996 by MBI Publishing Company,
PO Box 1, 729 Prospect Avenue, Osceola, WI
54020-0001 USA

© George Barris and David Fetherston, 1996

MBI Publishing Company books are also available at
discounts in bulk quantity for industrial or sales-
promotional use. For details write to Special Sales
Manager at Motorbooks International Wholesalers &
Distributors, 729 Prospect Avenue, PO Box 1, Osceola,
WI 54020-0001 USA.

Library of Congress Cataloging-in-Publication Data

Barris, George.
    Barris TV & movie cars / George Barris. David A.
Fetherston.
        p. cm.
    Includes index.
    ISBN 0-7603-0198-0
        1. Automobiles—United States.   2. Stage props
    —United States.   3. Barris, George.   I.
    Fetherston, David.   II. Title.
    TL23.B287   1996
    629.222'092—dc20   96-8847

On the front cover: One of Hollywood's greats—
the *Batmobile.*

On the frontispiece: Detail of an embroidered jacket
featuring some of "King George's" TV and movie cars.

On the title page: The *Batmobile* with Adam West as
"Batman."

On the back cover: These posters are from some of the
hot rod movies for which Barris built cars and stunt
vehicles in the 1950s; one of the most famous vehicles
to come out of the Barris shop—*the Munster Koach.*

Printed in Hong Kong

Contents

Acknowledgments 6

Chapter One   **George Barris at Work in the World of Sound and Image**   7

Chapter Two   **Action and Adventure TV Shows and Movies**   20
Batman
The Car
Dick Tracy
Fireball 500
Hardcastle and McCormick
Jurassic Park
Knight Rider
Mannix
The Silencers

Chapter Three   **Comedy on TV and in the Movies**   54
The Beverly Hillbillies
The Flintstones
The Good Guys
The Many Loves of Dobie Gillis
The Munsters
My Mother the Car
The Van

Chapter Four   **Romance in the Movies**   76
For Those Who Think Young
High School Confidential
Marriage on the Rocks
SuperVan

Chapter Five   **Musical and Youth TV Shows and Movies**   90
The Bugaloos
Easy Come, Easy Go
Good Times
Groovy
Out of Sight
Romp
Village of the Giants

Chapter Six   **Car and Hot Rod Movies**   106
Hot Rod Gang
Mag Wheels
Pit Stop
Race with Destiny
Thunder Alley

Chapter Seven   **Specialty Vehicles**   116
The Beach Boys' Mini Surfer
Elvis Presley's Limo
Paul Revere and the Raiders' Coach
The Voxmobile

Index   128

Acknowledgments

First I thank my wife, Shirley, for her many years of support and as a partner, for designing interiors and helping to create ideas for many of the movie cars that we built.

I would also like to recognize contributions made by the many people who have worked with me at the shop on all these extraordinary vehicles over the last forty-six years. Without their skill, knowledge, and dedication we could never have kept the cameras rolling.

George Barris

The quote from Jay Leno encapsulates my childhood memories of watching movies to enjoy the cars, far more than the stars, and almost always it was the Barris cars I wanted to see. George Barris was assuredly the right man in Hollywood at a time when the stars were aligned and allowed him to create film magic.

This is the second in a series of Barris books and what amazes me now that I have come to know and understand George is his capacity to accomplish so much creative work in the many different layers of his business enterprises, from car builder to stuntman, movie producer, and even as an actor.

This book once again allows us to look over George's shoulders back across nearly fifty years at the cars he has created so far during his extraordinary life building unique wheeled "stars" for the silver screen. Thanks go first to George for allowing this project to happen, to Tony Thacker, Greg Sharp, Greg Williams, and Ron Main for being editorial angels, and to the production staff at Fetherston Publishing, Ben Fetherston, Gloria Fetherston, and Nanette Simmons, for their research, ideas, and support.

David Fetherston

■

**"While other kids watched TV to see the stars,
I watched TV to see the Barris cars."**
Jay Leno

Chapter One

George Barris at Work in the World of Sound and Image

George Barris at Work in the World of Sound and Image

The beginning of the twentieth century brought with it massive strides in human endeavor and improvements for the quality and enjoyment of life. The telephone linked neighbor with neighbor. Airplanes ushered in the era of fast, efficient travel. Advances in medical science healed the sick. As towns small and large were wired for electricity, life was changing for the better.

As technology blossomed, so did the desire for entertaining pastimes. Two of the most important of these pastimes were the movies and the automobile. Suddenly, films brought motor vehicles and actors together, often with hilarious results. Among the most memorable were Max Sennett's "Keystone Cops," a slapstick entourage of police officers who used the motorcar in ways previously unimagined. To this framework came Stan Laurel and Oliver Hardy, who destroyed Ford Model Ts in the most amazing ways. Their expendable stunt cars were some of the first built for movie work.

Other comedic actors followed Laurel and Hardy's lead, and by the mid-thirties, even the inimitable W. C. Fields was employing the motorcar to enhance his "shtick." In the classic golf film *The 300 Yard Drive*, the portly Fields employed an accessorized 1930 American Bantam Sedan as a platform from which to drive his golf balls! With its debut up on the silver screen, the marriage of both the automobile and the art of comedy was fast becoming a favorite format for American audiences and film directors.

George Barris with the *SuperVan*.

In 1933, director John Blystone took the automobile to another level when he produced a reel of celluloid for Twentieth Century Fox called *My Lips Betray*. This trendsetting feature showcased a wildly customized Hispano-Suiza Sedanca-de-Ville—complete with oval headlights, an enormous front bumper, wheel discs, and oversized whitewalls. With widespread approval from theater-goers, the extravagantly restyled Hispano ushered in a new era of innovation in the film-making industry. Now, it was acknowledged that the automobile could be a competent player in its own right, not just as a prop but as a focal point of the story.

Naturally, the idea of driving at a high rate of speed became an important plot point in many of the movies to come. Pictures showcasing the sleek, low profiles of racing cars and the action-packed appeal of motorsports made their debut—introducing the exciting world of speed and beauty to audiences nationwide. Among the first of this new genre was a 1913 movie entitled *Race for Life*, starring the real-life racer Barney Oldfield.

The public responded at the box office, and soon a raft of new speedway movies roared into the cinema. Among the most notable of this fledgling racing theme was the 1932 hit *The Crowd Roars*, starring "tough guy" James Cagney. Two years later, actor Frankie Darro wowed movie audiences with a feature of his own called *Burn 'em Up Barnes*. In 1938, the classic flick called *Road Demon* captured imaginations and firmly cemented the union of

7

In the 1959 Alfred Hitchcock movie *North By Northwest*, a police car is mashed between Cary Grant's Mercedes-Benz sports roadster and a '47 Ford driven by Eva Marie Saint. For this scene the Barris shop constructed aluminum panels for the front and rear of the Ford police car so it would crumple more easily.

George provided cars for Alfred Hitchcock to use in his movie production of H. G. Wells' classic *The Time Machine*. The street scene needed a futuristic look so George used Bob Metz's wildly finned 1950 Buick custom and Shirley Barris's red candy custom 1958 Thunderbird (out of view in this shot).

automobile and motion-picture camera. By the decade's end, the motorized machine known as the "car" was viewed by Hollywood dream-makers as more than just a mere hunk of sheet metal and rubber, but a contrivance with a multi-dimensional appeal (and character) all its own.

But the best was yet to come! The fifties brought with it a fresh crop of auto-related movies which got even wilder, weirder, and "way-out." By then, the age of the hot rod movie had arrived with a vengeance. Over the next eight years, numerous motion-picture releases glorified the exploits of gasoline-powered youth. With titles like *The Cool Hot Rod* in 1953, *Hot Rod Girl* in 1956, *Hot Rod Rumble* in 1957, and *Hot Rod Gang* in 1958, the tentative acts of cruising portrayed during the developing years of America's cinema were quickly forgotten.

To supply the motor machinery required for these new teenage exploitation flicks, producers turned to the most obvious source: hot rod and custom car builders. Fortunately, the Barris brothers of Barris Kustoms were already well known in their custom car shop in Lynnwood, California, and by 1955 already had several of their creations featured in films. The customized curves of their famous *Hirohata Mercury* had dazzled audiences in the movie *Running Wild*, stealing the show (for car buffs) from actress Mamie Van Doren.

The growing demands of the movie industry required Barris to expand his business, creating a branch which would specialize in customized vehicles for the studios. Aware of his credentials, director Leslie Martinson approached Barris with a proposal in 1957: He was looking for a custom car to appear in his new film called *Hot Car Girl* (also known as *Hot Rod Girl*). Barris had just the ticket—a custom 1956 Ford convertible he had already built for Frank Monteleone.

Within a short time, there was a new customer knocking on his door: the emerging industry called television. Among his first offerings for this new medium was a *Playhouse 90* segment for which Barris supplied a '50 Ford built at his shop by Hershel "Junior" Conway.

With television producers established as customers, the Barris brothers' first venture into stunt vehicles was right around the corner. In 1957, Metro-Goldwyn-Mayer began preparing a production called *High School Confidential* with George and his brother Sam commissioned to

George supplied his own Dodge Hemi-powered roadster for the TV series *Window on Main Street* starring Robert Young. Everyone survived this crash scene.

build their first movie stunt cars. A key gimmick in the movie featured a "chicken race" in which one vehicle would be destroyed in a rollover. A pair of '48 Chevrolet coupes were delivered to the shop and Sam customized them identically: tops chopped, rear quarter windows filled, and custom grilles fitted. As required by the script, one coupe was destroyed in the filming, the surviving backup is now owned by a collector. By 1958 Barris' custom work became so well known that his famed hot rod *Ala Kart* was prominently displayed on the movie poster for *Hot Rod Gang* (starring Gene Vincent and John Ashley).

The film industry built Barris Kustom Shop's reputation for specialty cars and provided the keystone for garnering additional motion picture work. Along with these movie projects came a new onslaught of enthusiastic customers: the stars and their cars. Still, the backbone of Barris Kustoms was the building of custom cars and hot rods for their regular clientele. Projects ranged from simple repainting jobs to the assembly of crowd-pleasing automobiles created strictly for shows.

Unfortunately, a fire nearly put an end to the Barris Kustom business in 1957. The devastation was astounding. Along with the shop and all of its equipment, fourteen customized automobiles were destroyed, including a one-off magnesium- bodied custom Jaguar owned by boxer Archie Moore and an XK-120 belonging to Jayne Mansfield. With no insurance on the operation, the future looked bleak for Barris; but he managed to not only rebuild his business but achieve far greater success than he could ever have imagined.

The caped crusaders, Batman and Robin, head out in the *Batmobile*.

In 1959, Alfred Hitchcock featured Cary Grant, Eva Marie Saint, James Mason, and Martin Landau in the high-suspense *North By Northwest*. A scene called for a car chase in which a police car would be smashed between Cary Grant's Mercedes-Benz sports roadster and Eva Marie Saint's 1947 Ford. To accommodate the film's needs, the Barris shop fabricated soft aluminum panels and bumpers to replace the stock bodywork for the rear of the

Mercedes, the nose (and tail) of the Ford police car, and the nose of the '47 Ford. Crumpling easier than factory steel panels, these modified parts were used to produce a more impressive crash scene. The idea worked perfectly: the chase scene went off without a hitch (no pun intended). Cars crunched dramatically and no stunt drivers were injured.

Hitchcock turned to Barris again. This time in 1960 for his production of H. G. Wells' classic, *The*

Time Machine, Hitchcock needed to portray a futuristic look for street scenes that would take place in the not so distant future of 1980. Barris delivered Bob Metz's wildly finned 1950 Buick custom along with Shirley Barris' red candy custom 1958 Thunderbird. The scene portrayed an atomic blast which destroyed everything on Earth. Fortunately, the special effects of the sixties saved these beautiful vehicles from destruction: a quick splicing of film joined shots of the real cars with a matching scale model of the set using toy cars. Thus, the cars survived unscathed.

In 1959, a new teenage comedy graced the small screen in the hit show *The Many Loves of Dobie Gillis*. The producers urgently needed a specialty car for the show. Once again, Barris came to the rescue. Like an automotive magician, he pulled a wild car out of his hat by repainting the old Chrisman Bonneville coupe with thirty coats of diamond-sparkle pearl-white lacquer—accented with kandy-tangerine on the roof and side panels. Barris topped off the redux by adding a fully chromed Oldsmobile engine and new wheels, renaming his new creation the *XMSC-210*.

In that same year, Barris turned his attention to winning a highly coveted hot rod award for his personal 1927 T hot rod roadster—built with a Dodge Hemi V-8 engine. The roadster had previously been leased out for the television series *Window on Main Street,* starring Robert Young. Barris rebuilt the hot rod and succeeded in winning the famous Oakland Roadster Show's "World's Most Beautiful Roadster Award." The award had been given to him twice before, but this was the first time it was awarded for a roadster that he owned.

The sixties brought the Barris shop further into the limelight with the creation of a remote-controlled vehicle for the Jerry Lewis movie *The Patsy*. The car was created from a Beldone show car whose trunks, doors, and hood had been re-engineered to be operated by remote control. Lewis, who played a witless bellboy, had quite a time trying to keep parts of the car opened or closed. Trunk, doors, hood—all appeared to have minds of their own!

By this time, the Barris Kustom Shop moved from Lynnwood to a new location at Riverside Drive in North Hollywood where it still operates. Television work continued to come in in the early sixties when CBS producer Paul Henning asked Barris to build a jalopy for a new comedy series called *The Beverly*

George modified the old Ford Beldone showcar to create a comic remote-controlled vehicle for the Jerry Lewis movie *The Patsy*.

The *Munster Koach.*

Hillbillies. The program would center around the Clampetts, a back woods Ozark family who struck it rich with "black gold" and subsequently relocated to Beverly ("Hills, that is") in a battered 1921 Oldsmobile "truck." After a serious search, Barris found a suitable vehicle in the back of an old feed store in Fontana, California. With the addition of the Barris hillbilly truck, Henning's irreverent comedy became an instant success and went on to become one of CBS's longest running sitcoms.

Movie and television work kept Barris busy, but whenever he could find the time he would tinker around with his own designs. One such work was a superbly restyled 1963 Buick Riviera; its cantilever roof and brilliant candy apple red paint work were stunning. Unfortunately, it was repainted within a couple of months for use in the movie *For Those Who Think Young.* The director, Leslie Martinson, had seen

the Buick, loved it, but wanted it painted white. Barris obliged and James Darren and Bob Denver used it in the movie as their surf wagon and cruiser.

Barris discovered over the years that the movie and television industry, with its insatiable capacity for using special vehicles, had one problem: more often than not, it wanted a finished product immediately, if not sooner. This constant demand for excellence on short notice created a dilemma for Barris. He was aware that building an original vehicle to suit the production was the best method, but time constraints did not give him the time to build a special vehicle from the ground up. Instead, Barris had to use his imagination to create vehicles from cars that already existed.

The *Batman* television series was an example. Bob Kane, who produced the Batman script for ABC Television, desperately wanted a bat car . . . and fast.

For the rock band Paul Revere and the Raiders, George built this twin Pontiac GTO-powered stage coach-power unit to pull a traditional 18th century stagecoach.

Production was scheduled to start in three weeks! Undaunted, Barris created a wild *Batmobile* using the old Lincoln Futura show car. The fantastic design won instant approval and soon more movie companies were knocking on his door.

One such company was Universal Studios which wanted a wacky but functional vehicle for their new *Munsters* TV series. Without missing a beat, Barris produced a concept sketch of the *Munster Koach*. It met with immediate approval from Universal, but Barris had only twenty-one days to deliver! By this time Barris was accustomed to tight deadlines; he quickly reorganized his staff to work around-the-clock in order to deliver the *Koach* on time. The result was a spectacular vehicle that combined hot-rodding with antique stagecoach styling. The combination of old and new produced a "family car" which gen-

erations of *Munsters* fans have come to recognize and love.

Within a year and a half Barris was commissioned to build yet another vehicle for the Munster family. This time, it was to be an outlandish combination of hot rod, coffin, and dragster. It was dubbed the *Drag-u-la* and Grandpa Munster's affectionate quip described it best: "You can go in it or you can *go* in it."

The demand for Barris' work increased and by this time even auto manufacturers sought out his unique work. Among them was Ford Motor Company which commissioned him to construct a series of custom cars for their Ford Custom Caravan promotion. With Barris as the star of the tour, this racy clique of Ford show-stoppers traveled the nation and participated in car shows. Like every other star, Barris was sought out by autograph

For the Cinema J Productions 1968 release of *A Boy, A Girl*, George built this wildly painted, but basically stock, 1967 Pontiac Firebird convertible. Starring Dino Martin and Airion Fromer, the movie was about young love in the swinging sixties. George created a theme for the paint scheme which used the male and female signs on the doors along with a crazy psychedelic paint job of flames and swirls over a pale blue base.

seekers and fans everywhere. Such was his fame that even the April 1965 cover of *Hot Rod* magazine featured his *Surf Woody* on the cover as one of the most memorable custom automobiles of the year.

Through the rest of 1965 Barris was kept running in overdrive as he created his unusual automobiles for the television and movie industries: A vintage Porter touring car became the talkative star of the latest series, *My Mother the Car*. For *Village of the Giants*, a hot rod was rigged by Barris to disintegrate when a giant teenager stepped on it. Director Jack Donohue ordered two cars for his Frank Sinatra/Dean Martin film, *Marriage on the Rocks*. Although the new Ford Mustang had just arrived on the market, Barris sliced up one of the racy coupes, rebodied it and created the *Zebra Mustang* for this movie. The second car for the film was a superb custom Thunderbird built to look crisp with wild paint and molded body work.

The following year, four major movie and entertainment projects were undertaken, including a Plymouth Barracuda fastback converted into the *Fireball 500* roadster (featured in the movie starring Annette Funicello, Fabian, and Frankie Avalon); a custom Mercury Colony Park station wagon was created for the Dean Martin movie *The Silencers,* and a zebra-striped Jeep J-series truck was customized for Ivan Tors' new MGM TV series, *Daktari*.

The most challenging job of the year was the one-off radical music stagecoach for the rock-and-roll band Paul Revere and the Raiders. To meet this unusual request, an innovative twin GTO-powered unit that used 800hp was created to pull a traditional eighteenth-century stagecoach. The resulting vehicle became known as the *Raiders' Coach* and toured the show car circuit for the next two years. In addition to these appearances, the celebrated vehicle appeared

This 1967 Firebird convertible was repainted with flower and music motifs for a song called "Daisy Fields" sung by the group The Celebration on the *Romp* TV special.

with the group on numerous record covers, stage shows, and publicity tours.

The Barris shop rumbled into 1967 with some of their best work yet. To start off the year, a raucous Buick-engined *ZZR* hot rod was designed for the movie *Out of Sight* and a beautiful custom Oldsmobile Toronado roadster fashioned for the TV detective series *Mannix*. A customized Dodge Charger fastback followed for use in the film *Thunder Alley*, starring Fabian and former "Mousketeer" Annette Funicello, and then a pair of custom Mustang convertibles were done up for pop stars Sonny and Cher. The Mustangs were used in the duo's first movie *Good Times* and later toured the show circuit. In addition to his custom car duties behind the scenes, Barris punctuated the year by appearing in front of the cameras as well. A segment of the movie *Pit Stop* was filmed at his workshop and

featured Barris in the role he knew best: custom car builder. Scenes included his Buick Wildcat, *The Calico Surfer*, and the partially constructed *Alvin's Safety Car*.

Barris wrapped up the late sixties with three major projects, beginning with the completion of *Alvin's Safety Car* for the *Alvin the Chipmunk and Friends* TV show. The car, a mix of custom and hot-rod touring, was used to promote driving safety to kids. A hippie-painted Firebird convertible produced for the Dean Martin Jr. movie *A Boy, A Girl* kept Barris busy, as did an antique taxi (a revamped 1924 Lincoln Touring car) created especially for the memorable television series *The Good Guys*.

The celluloid era of the seventies dawned with several new projects, the most notable being the TV show *Romp* starring Ryan O'Neal and Jimmy Durante. The pair required several special vehicles for use in the show, including a

The first *Batmobile* illustration.

The *Batmobile*, Batman, and George Barris: three Hollywood greats.

motor home that looked like a gargantuan boat, a comical police car, and a snappy GTO ragtop. The special requests didn't end there: *The Bugaloos* children's show asked for a lovable buggy which Barris built using a Volkswagen platform and a full custom buggy body. After that, the teenage series *Groovy* requested a couple of cars that would evoke the free spirit of youth. Barris Kustoms accommodated by building a pair of dune buggies that were used for beach racing and props when rock-and-roll artists appeared on the show. Barris even made a cameo appearance on *Groovy*, piloting one of his rides with host Mike Blodgett riding shotgun.

As the decade of flower power wore on, Barris augmented his work for the visual industries by creating custom automobiles for major celebrities and large corporations which required something "completely different." Among those fortunate enough to have had the pleasure of owning (and showing off) a Barris creation were Clint Eastwood, Elvis Presley, John Wayne, Buddy Hackett, Glen Campbell, Liberace, Dean Martin, Nancy Sinatra, Cher, Coca-Cola, Coppertone Suntan Lotion, Lipton Tea, and Campbell's Soup.

Once again, the music industry turned to Barris. This time it was Vox, maker of guitars, amplifiers, and drums, which decided to invest in its own unique promotional vehicle. As always, the ingenious Barris came through with a design that symbolized the music industry perfectly: a giant guitar-shaped masterpiece aptly dubbed the *Voxmobile*. As chief mascot in the instrument maker's advertising and publicity department, the eye-popping four-wheeler caught the attention of garage band hopefuls all across America.

In the late seventies, Barris signed a deal with Universal Studios' director Elliot Silverstein to build three cars for the soon-to-be-produced thriller *The Car*. The movie starred James Brolin and Kathleen Lloyd as the hapless inhabitants of a small Utah community besieged by the evil *Car*. Hell-bent on the complete annihilation of the town and the lead characters, the evil *Car* stole the show. Created from three Lincoln Mark IIIs which were converted into nefarious black coupes sporting raised fenders and massive grilles, this otherworldly adversary-on-wheels proved to one of Barris' most frightening designs.

During the eighties, Barris continued his relationship with the television and motion-

George built this "babe-mobile" Pontiac Firebird convertible for use by Mike Blodgett on the TV show *Groovy*.

picture industries by providing more and more photogenic phaetons. Most notable was the vehicle created for the TV series *Knight Rider*, which starred David Hasselhoff. Produced by Glen Larsen Productions for Universal Studios, the series ran for four years beginning in September 1982. The first black cars were built

For the TV series *The Good Guys* George created this antique taxi out of a 1924 Lincoln touring car. The main characters from the show can be seen from left to right, Bob Denver as Rufus Betterworth, Joyce Van Patten as Claudia Gramus, and Herb Edelman as Bert Gramus.

The *Voxmobile* appeared in many Vox advertisements with Jimmy Bryant, renowned as "The World's Fastest Guitarist." Jimmy is seen here with the Ford Cobra 289 V-8-powered *Voxmobile* before a photo session for a Vox. The roadster featured a hot rod–style chassis with a chromed drop tube axle up front and a regular coil spring rear suspension. On the road the *Voxmobile* had plenty of punch from the Cobra V-8 as the entire car weighed under 2,000lb.

by Universal but for the last two seasons of the show, a far more futuristic version of the Pontiac Firebird was specified.

The Barris version? A coupe complete with secondary driving position mounted low in the passenger seat to facilitate a hidden pilot!

To enhance the exterior, the body was revised with decorative wings and spoilers. The result was a Barris vehicle that embodied the concept of an autonomous being with a unique personality.

This could have marked the high point of any car customizer, but for Barris, it was only another stop on the journey. As the seventies gave way to the eighties and then to the nineties, the Barris shop continued producing its gasoline-powered art works. Among the latest innovations were the pink Auburn boat-tailed Speedster replica for the *Dick Tracy* movie and the foot-powered "stone" cars specially crafted for the big-screen version of the *Flintstones* cartoon.

How did Barris build "stone" cars? They were carved out of foam and then carefully molded to make working fiberglass replicas (one powered by Fred's and Barney's feet, the other by a small, concealed electric engine)!

For over four decades, George Barris and the amazing work coming out of the Barris Kustom shop has endured—captured for posterity on countless reels of film and videotape. His automotive creations have inspired movie audiences from around the world and continue to do so. His venture into the arena of custom cars has led him into a realms of both visual excitement and great physical demands. Not only has he been the creator of memorable custom cars, but also a stunt coordinator, actor, director, and film advisor. In the final analysis, George Barris' most notable movie achievement is that he delivers the goods time and time again, seemingly effortlessly, and continues to build the greatest movie cars to ever grace the silver screen.

■

"When I was a young man living in Philadelphia, I would read about this young man in California who would do incredible things, customizing cars and creating his own designs. A few years later, I made my way to California and into show business and had the pleasure of meeting George Barris, the young auto design genius. We've been friends ever since. George later customized and built cars for films in which I starred, and of course, my personal cars. He is, without a doubt, the *best* at what he does."
James Darren

Chapter Two

Action and Adventure TV Shows and Movies

Batman

Action/adventure movies and TV shows. Two black-and-white movie serials, fifteen episodes each in 1943 and 1949. Television series ran from 1964–66; William Dozier, producer; ABC. Full-length movie in 1966. TV series starred: Adam West as Batman, Burt Ward as Robin, Cesar Romero as the Joker, and Frank Gorshin as the Riddler.

For imaginative children glued to their television screens during the mid-sixties, nothing captured their imaginations more than the *Batmobile*. When kids played with their Matchbox cars, they dreamed of this speeding black beauty as it exited the Batcave at top speed—complete with flames shooting from its exhaust nozzle and the turbine whine of its jet engine.

When the "caped-crusader" and his loyal sidekick, Robin, invaded the airwaves in 1964,

Batman became an instant success. Using a three-dimensional comic book style with tongue always in cheek, it was a high-camp hit that soon had kids all across the country strapping on utility belts and sliding down banisters. ABC Television arranged international distribution to Australia and England, and then licensed it for translation into Japanese, French, German, Italian, and other languages. In 1966, the first *Batman* motion picture was produced as a direct

The Lincoln Futura was built in 1955 by Ghia in Italy to a design created by Lincoln-Mercury stylists in Dearborn, Michigan. The futuristic bubble-topped concept car was a big hit on the showcar circuit for several years after its release in 1955. Toward the latter part of the fifties, the car was used in the movie *It Started with a Kiss*, which was about an Air Force sergeant (Glenn Ford), his new bride (Debbie Reynolds), and a fabulous car, the Lincoln Futura.

The *Batmobile* was everything the TV show producers wanted. Gotham City would never be the same again! The *Batmobile* had all the working wiz-bang gizmos the producers had begged for. It looked like the car that Batman would drive, and had enough pep, with its Lincoln V-8 engine, to make it faster than a flying bat. The *Batmobile* was also an instant hit with viewers of the new show and over the next thirty years it was made into dozens of different toy and model kits for kids worldwide to enjoy. George has over fifty different toy *Batmobiles* in his own collection.

Just before the show was released George was asked by *TV GUIDE* to do a publicity stunt with the *Batmobile* for the cover of the magazine. George drove the *Batmobile* down the Hollywood Freeway with the Batchutes fully opened into the wind behind the car, while the magazine photographer shot the photos from a freeway overpass. These days it would be an impossible task (except perhaps at 7A.M. on a Sunday morning) because of the traffic pressure on this freeway.

spin-off of the television show. It featured the Barris *Batmobile*.

The history of the *Batmobile* is a fun-filled and interesting story. Batman evolved from the forties' DC comic book cartoon character into a real life action TV hit of the sixties. In the comic book, Batman drove various automobiles—but mostly they were comically shaped and did not represent a production automobile. A befitting

The *Batmobile* was featured in many different scenes in the show and performed a huge variety of stunts; drag racing was among its activities. Here, at the famed old Irwindale Raceway, the *Batmobile* smokes the track with a full-blown cloud of movie smoke from tires and jet turbine exhaust. Stunts like this were faked with many types of movie tricks as the producers did not want to endanger or break anything on the *Batmobile* that would stop production.

The interior of the *Batmobile* was filled with crimefighting tools including a rocket launcher, Batphones, antitheft devices, radios, a Batscope, escape tools, a Detect-a-scope, laser gun controls, flashing lights, sound and weapon systems, and a remote TV camera and screen. The photo shows the interior of one of the second generation *Batmobiles* that George built as a back up for the show and to use on the show car circuit.

Stored in the Batcave, the *Batmobile* was always ready for instant use by the Dynamic Duo. Here Batman steps aboard without using the door.

The popularity of the show and the *Batmobile* necessitated George building a series of replicas to satisfy the growing requests from auto show promoters, museums, and movie events. From the original car he pulled a set of full body molds and made five show car versions. Here the crew works on finishing one of those cars in the back lot at the Barris shop. George can be seen working on the headlight. The remains of George's old *X.P.A.K. 400* air car can be seen stacked up behind the *Batmobile*.

Batmobile was needed and Bob Kane, the originator and script writer of the TV show, had a big problem: time. ABC was starting production within twenty-one days! Bob called George Barris and presented him with the problem.

As the story goes, Barris had recently purchased the 1955 Lincoln Futura dream car from the Ford Motor Company after it had been used in the 1959 Glenn Ford, Debbie Reynolds movie *It Started With a Kiss*. Designed by Lincoln-Mercury and built in Italy by the coachbuilder Ghia, the Futura was a great hit on the Ford show car circuit during the fifties. Barris came up with a concept using the Futura as the basis for the new *Batmobile*.

Unfortunately, Barris had less than three weeks to get the *Batmobile* designed, built and delivered. He spent an entire day at the drawing board refining his ideas and the following morn-

ing called Bob Kane to show him the sketches. Kane took the drawings to ABC Television and they gave the project the "thumbs up." With barely two weeks work time, Barris and his loyal crew of Bud Kunz and Les Tompkins began burning the midnight oil.

To create the *Batmobile*, the basic shape of the Futura was left as it was. However, the rest of the car received radical modifications. The nose and tail were completely reworked and the sides were changed so much that the original Futura was unrecognizable. The nose was restyled with a bat theme: hooded headlights, a peaked nose, and nostril-like hood scoops. The hood was bubbled up as it pulled back from the twin nostril scoops. The "bat look" was continued in the design of the headlights, with "eyes" that pulled back into what appeared to be a pair of ears— bat ears! Following this theme, the twin-meshed

The Car

Mystery/action/thriller movie in 1977; Elliot Silverstein, director; Universal Studios. Starred: James Brolin, Kathleen Lloyd, John Marley, John Rubinstein, Ronny Cox, and R. G. Armstrong.

When film director Elliot Silverstein looked over the script for his next movie *The Car*, he immediately thought of George Barris and what kind of vehicle he could build to make the movie memorable. Set in Utah and filmed on location in Zion National Park and the small towns of Hurricane, St. George, and Kanab, it was an auto horror flick that featured a driverless car possessed by evil forces.

As per the script, the sinister *Car* had the ability to change the weather, never needed gas, and ran over as many people as it could. When it arrived on the scene, a disturbing wind kicked up with monstrous force. The demon *Car's* only weakness was that it could not cross hallowed ground. After killing off half of the town, the cruiser is finally stopped by Wade, the sheriff's deputy. He sets a trap, and the *Car* shoots off a cliff and explodes, finally laying to rest its evil spirits. This stunt destroyed three of the five fiberglass replicas.

Barris took a Lincoln Mark III coupe and fabricated an entirely new body over the Lincoln's substructure. His work gave the *Car* an evil look with puffed up fenders, a chopped roof, amber windows, a deeply recessed grille, and headlights. Intense work, the project called for a team of twelve to get all six cars finished for the movie's production deadline. Construction of the initial car took eight weeks as the project required hand fabrication in steel and the installation of special stunt and safety devices.

Famous Hollywood stunt coordinator Everett Creach made up the specifications for the *Car* that included a locked rear axle with 4.11 gears (in order to spin the car out easier), heavy-duty double shocks, double bumpers front and rear (for ramming), a full roll cage, reinforced seats, and a five-point racing seat safety harness. Comfortable with these heavy-duty features, stuntman Creach worked the movie *Cars* over solidly—totally destroying the fiberglass replicas in several major crashes.

For *The Car* George built a main car and five replicas. Using a Lincoln Mark III coupe he laid out all the changes in tape before the metal fabricators started on their part of the job. Interestingly, *The Car* was chopped but George also raised the hip line so the side windows became even shorter.

The body men had quite a task to get the new sheet metal right. Except for the roof skin, all the sheet metal was new. Once this first unit was completed, a set of fiberglass molds were taken and the five stunt cars were built using fiberglass components.

This photo, taken on the set, shows both cameras shooting simultaneously, giving the editor two angles to cut together to make one action scene. *The Car* is sliding around trying to run over the two actors sitting down on the right.

The Car was rigged with a platform and a turntable mounted on it. The camera was mounted inside the car to allow filming of the actress beside the car while it was traveling at high speed and appearing to drag her alongside.

Road surface didn't stop *The Car* from chasing after its victims. Here Deputy Sheriff Wade dives for cover among the rocks as *The Car* comes charging over the ridge in pursuit.

One of the stunt *Cars* was destroyed in this scene when the sheriff attempted to blow it up on a lonely stretch of highway.

The completed *Cars* were large and sinister-looking. Painted in gloss black with only a touch of chrome for the bumpers, they had a mystical, evil appearance.

The film crew watches tensely as *The Car* tries to drive Sheriff Wade in his AMC Matador off the mountain road. The camera man is on a boom that puts him above the action so he can get his shot without interfering with the two vehicles.

Dick Tracy

Cops-and-robbers action movie in 1990; Warren Beatty, producer/director; Disney Studios. Starred: Warren Beatty, Madonna, Al Pacino, Glenne Headly, Charlie Korsmo, Dustin Hoffman, Seymour Cassel, Mandy Patinkin, James Keane, William Forsyth, Charles Durning, Paul Sorbino, Dick Van Dyke, James Caan, Michael J. Pollard, Estelle Parsons, R. J. Armstrong, Kathy Bates, and Mary Woronov.

Dick Tracy films have been around since the late 1930s, when Republic Pictures made Saturday matinee serials showcasing the famous cartoon detective. This first serial was called *Dick Tracy's G-Men* and was produced in fifteen episodes. RKO pictures revived the Tracy image after World War II and made four Dick Tracy movies with a series of famous and not-so-famous actors playing Tracy. Some of these films were *Dick Tracy Versus Cueball*, *Dick Tracy Meets Gruesome*, and *Dick Tracy's Dilemma*. While crime formats have come and gone over the years, Dick Tracy has always been there. And who could ever forget Dick Tracy's two-way wrist radio/television?

The 1990 Dick Tracy movie was directed by its star, Warren Beatty. The movie was more of a parody on the standard cops-and-robbers' theme than a real thriller. Al Pacino made an appearance as the villain with vampy Madonna and Glenne Headly each doing bang-up jobs.

For this full-scale comic book production, George created the special car that Madonna's character, Breathless, was to drive. Using an Auburn Boattailed Speedster kit, George assembled a bright pink roadster. He included chrome wire wheels, wide white walls, and all the accessories required to make this Auburn replica look dynamic.

George built this small-block Chevrolet V-8-powered bright pink Auburn Speedster for Breathless to drive in the movie as she chased after Dick Tracy. After the movie the car was taken on a national tour; the car carries advertising for the movie.

Fireball 500

Action/romance movie in 1966; Burt Topper, producer; William Asher, director; American International.
Starred: Frankie Avalon, Annette Funicello, Fabian, Julie Parish, Chill Wills, and Harvey Lembeck.

The poster for *Fireball 500* featured the bold headline: "They live from spinout to crackup and they love as fast as they can get it!" More appropriate words could not have described this entry into the teenage racing genre. The basic plot: popular teen idols Fabian and Frankie Avalon compete for glory on the racetrack and for the affection of Annette Funicello. At the same time, they unknowingly transport moonshine whiskey. The film mixed music, action, romance, and a host of conflicting characters against the backdrop of annual championship stock car racing. Typical of the 1960s period teenage racing formats, this high-octane production was rife with auto action that included chicken races, moonshine chases, and just plain balls-out crash-and-burn racing.

The main feature car for *Fireball 500* was a highly customized 1966 Plymouth Barracuda that Barris Kustoms restyled into the *Super Styling Experimental Roadster (SSXR)*. The Barracuda was customized using radical body surgery; the roof

A completely new hood and nose was hand-formed for the roadster with a Pontiac GTO-like peak in the center. Twin oval grille openings were formed with a stamped mesh grille surrounding the oval headlight openings. The hood featured a pair of intake panels which would later be filled with four chromed ram tubes on each side. This photo also shows the new twin cockpits and the new cowl before the twin windshields were installed.

George took a new 1966 Plymouth Barracuda fastback and with it created the *Fireball 500* roadster. Plans called for a completely new nose, the roof to be sliced off, and dual cowl windshields. George is seen here with Carl Cooley, his project engineer, looking over the engineering drawings for the roadster at the shop in North Hollywood.

This rear shot of the completed roadster shows the flying headrest fairings, twin sidepipes, and custom rear end with its full width taillight assembly. It is also interesting to note how many crew are in this photo, and this is only part of the crew who worked on each scene.

was sliced off and a dual cockpit was formed to give the appearance of a racing roadster. The dual cowl was fabricated in sheet metal with twin streamlined Plexiglas windshields and matching formed headrests flowing out onto the rear deck.

But that was only a small part of the total customizing work that went into the Barracuda. The Barris shop created a completely new nose section with two oval openings, a pointed center section, four hidden rectangular Cibie French headlights, and a brushed aluminum extrusion

tube grille. The hood was modified with a pair of Ram-Thrust inlet tubes that were stylized into a cold air induction system. The rear end was modified with extended rear fenders and slim-line vertical taillights. To complete the effect, both rear fenders were extended 4in and blended to gracefully match both the new sculptured side panels and the revised rear end treatment, which also included a new trunk lid grille.

The little details were refined by Barris as well. Both door handles were shaved and replaced with pull-down handles contoured to

Many of the driving scenes in the movie were shot on the sound stage with film projected onto the background—it appeared that Frankie Avalon was actually driving the roadster. It would seem that this photo was taken before or after filming of this scene as everyone is laughing. This kind of film work on a sound stage was quintessential of the movie industry production techniques in the sixties.

match the shape of the body panels. Taillights were Frenched and matched with a set of high-mounted stoplights, both fitted right into the headrests. The wheel openings were modified with fully radiused openings on the rear and modified semi-radiused up front. In the rubber department, Barris replaced all four wheels with steel-rimmed, cast aluminum centered Raders capped with 700/12.50x13 Firestone tires. More than just a pretty face, the *SSXR* was powered by a 426 Plymouth Hemi with a four-speed transmission. A pair of AI Racing sidepipes added flair.

To complement the *Fireball 500* title, the Barris body shop finished the roadster with a spectacular Fireheat paint scheme. According to Barris, "the job took four painters six days to get the colors blended from fireheat pearl white on the nose, to candy

burgundy on the rear section." The paint transitioned from a white pearl nose into murano gold, candy tangerine, candy red, and finally candy burgundy on the rear. Apparently, forty coats of color and clear went into creating this wild paint scheme.

With Frankie Avalon at the wheel, the *SSXR* was used in both location and studio scenes. It was a fully functional movie car and was one of the major attractions of the movie and central to the main storyline. For the flick, Barris also built a replica of Richard Petty's #43 1966 Plymouth NASCAR racer. This racer was quickly picked up by the AMT corporation for a model kit, released as the "*Fireball 500* Plymouth." After the movie was completed, Barris took both the Petty racer and the *SSXR* on tour for appearances at movie theaters, drag strips, and car shows.

Annette Funicello is seen here with the completed *Super Styling Experimental Roadster (SSXR)*. The huge (for the era) Rader wheels capped with Firestone tires can be seen along with the final flat-bar stock grille which hid the headlights set back in the grille openings.

The completed *SSXR* was a great hit and well worth the hundreds of hours it took to create. The *SSXR* is still around and functional, and is part of a Midwest Mopar collection.

This photo shows two of the cars from *Fireball 500* parked outside the Barris shop on Riverside Drive in North Hollywood. Not only did George build the *SSXR* Plymouth, he also created a replica of Richard Petty's #43 Satellite hardtop NASCAR racer for the movie. The Petty car was used to tow the *SSXR* roadster to many movie promotions and car shows in Southern California after the movie was completed. Note the second billboard on the building; it is for American Sunroof Corporation a company that was started in the back of the Barris shop by Heinz Prechter. Today, it is a huge Detroit-based corporation which builds many of the convertibles for General Motors along with development engineering for companies including Rolls-Royce, Porsche, Mitsubishi, and Toyota.

■

"I can jump and fly wheels
anywhere, but George makes cars
and bikes look beautiful."
Evel Knievel

Hardcastle and McCormick

*Television detective/adventure series ran from September 1983 to July 1986; Paramount. Starred:
Brian Keith as Judge Milton G. Hardcastle, Daniel Hugh-Kelly as Mark "Skid" McCormick,
Mary Jackson as Sarah Wicks, and John Hancock as Lieutenant Michael Delaney.*

Hardcastle and McCormick was a television series that involved a retired, but athletic, judge who decides to track down criminals who beat the rap in his courtroom. Hardcastle is a bit of a rebel himself, evidenced by the Hawaiian shirts worn under his juristic robes. Not afraid of using unconventional methods, the aging Hardcastle looks for someone to assist him in his mission.

He recruits a two-time car thief and former racing car driver by the name of Mark "Skid" McCormick. Their relationship is based on the premise that if Skid plays it right, the judge will eventually get him off the hook.

Enter another custom automobile built by carmeisters George Barris and Mike Fennel: Hardcastle and McCormick are equipped with a fetching red *Manta* sports car powered by a small block Chevrolet V-8 engine mounted on a custom, heavy-duty chassis. With it, the stars tool around town at high speed and chase the bad guys. Appropriately, the *Manta* license plate reads "De Judge."

The show exhibited a fast-paced mix of wisecracks, automobile crashes, and judicial interference—with the zippy *Manta* crashing repeatedly as the pair pursue a variety of criminals around the crowded boulevards of Los Angeles, California.

George is seen here with star Daniel Hugh-Kelly during the filming of *Hardcastle and McCormick*. Hugh-Kelly played Mark "Skid" McCormick, the judge's car-stealing assistant. The *Manta* was asked to perform many feats and took a good bashing during its years on the set. George was always on hand to keep this brilliant red sports coupe running and looking like nothing had ever happened to it. Ertl, the toy manufacturer, produced kits and metal toys of the *Hardcastle and McCormick Manta*.

Jurassic Park

Action/suspense movie in 1993; Steven Spielberg, director; Universal. Starred: Sam Neill, Laura Dern, Jeff Goldblum, Ariana Richards, Joseph Mazzello, Samuel L. Jackson, Bob Peck, and Richard Attenborough.

Jurassic Park was based on a novel written by Michael Crichton. Steven Spielberg directed the screenplay version and parlayed the concept into the worlds' biggest grossing movie hit of all time. In 1993, it collected a total of seven Academy Awards.

A hold-onto-your-seat thriller about a tourist attraction set on an island off the coast of Costa Rica, *Jurassic Park* featured an unusual cast of characters, both human and reptilian. In the film, the main antagonists are a cantankerous group of genetically cloned dinosaurs (created in three dimensions, courtesy of Silicon Graphics and computer animation). As generally happens in all movies where the animals "run amok," the hungry beasts escape from their confines and seek out the scientists and visitors for a snack.

In this theme park, the main ride-along attraction is equipped with driverless Ford Explorers. The Fords were designed by John Bell at Industrial Light and Magic in San Rafael, California, and built at the Universal Studios workshops in Burbank. Barris' work with the movie was to create the illusion of the Explorers driving themselves as they move along a pre-set course on the park "ride."

To achieve this, a remote driver position was built into the Explorer's cargo area. A new rack was constructed between the rear wheel wells, and a power boat-style tensioned cable steering system was installed that attached to the main steering column. A set of remote foot controls for acceleration and braking were also installed, while tinted rear windows hid the driver during the filming. A television camera was mounted on the upper dash panel and provided an image in the rear compartment on a small monitor used by the stunt driver to navigate the vehicle.

George demonstrates the Explorer's remote steering installation. On the left are the foot controls for acceleration and braking and the TV monitor to see ahead is on the floor in front of him. With the windows tinted and the stunt driver dressed in black, the Explorer could be driven anywhere and appear to be driverless.

For *Jurassic Park*, a series of four-door Ford Explorers were converted for use on a theme park ride by the workshops at Universal Studios. The paintwork was created by John Bell to look like a mixture of dinosaur skin and camouflage and the Explorers were trimmed with off-road accessories including driving lights and spotlights, light bars, alloy wheels, vista roof, and a remote TV.

Knight Rider

Television action/adventure series ran from September 1982 to August 1986; Glen Larsen Productions, producer; Universal Studios. Starred: David Hasselhoff as Michael Knight, Edward Mulhare as Devon Miles, Patricia McPherson as Bonnie Barstow, and William Daniels as the voice of KITT.

Knight Rider played on the premise of a dying multimillionaire who saves a wounded undercover cop. In the show, David Hasselhoff's character Michael Young took a gunshot to the face and underwent reconstructive facial surgery. Indebted to benefactor Wilton Knight, he assumed a new identity as Michael Knight and renewed his work of fighting injustice. To aid him in his exploits, Wilton has developed an incredible supercar at his company, Knight Industries. The high-tech rig is officially known as the *Knight Industries Two-Thousand*, or *KITT* for short.

This Pontiac Trans-Am was more than just another flashy speedster; the customized cre-ation was impervious to attack and could run at speeds up to 300mph. At the touch of a button, it could leap through the air. As part of the crime-fighting package, on-board armaments included flame-throwers and smoke bombs. An overly talkative computer with its own personality was installed into the dash, which regularly dispensed advice. The car also possessed the ability to see through walls, smoke, and around corners. If that was not enough for an ordinary television supercar, it could also read minds.

The series ran for four seasons and Barris was asked to build new cars for the third season. The first two seasons featured a single black

The first version of *KITT* was built at Universal Studios based on an F-bodied Pontiac Trans Am Firebird. This model, along with six stunt versions, was used for the first two seasons of the show. The only external sign that *KITT* was anything different from a regular Trans Am was the red strobe lights fitted into the nose. They would flash and strobe back and forth as the car spoke or sensed where its "master" Michael Knight was located.

For the third season George created a more complex and active version of *KITT* featuring movable spoilers, wings, scoops, and air brakes. This process took about eight weeks to complete, working day and night. Much of the bodywork was functional with air brakes that popped out, wings that raised up, and bodywork that extended.

The complexity of the new car included a nose that popped forward, a spoiler that jumped up, and a roof that folded down to form a roadster. All of these pieces were electrically driven and remotely controlled.

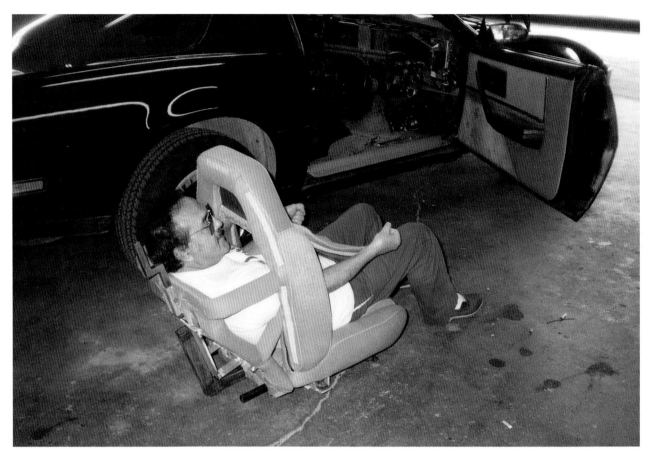

In order for the car to appear to drive itself, George created a right-hand driving position with a second steering wheel that sat below the dash. He then reconfigured the passenger seat so that the stunt driver could just see over the cowl but was hidden in and behind the passenger seat as he did the driving.

Trans-Am that had been built by the prop department at Universal Studios. For the 1985 season, Barris redid the car with more extravagant additions, including wings, scoops, and a convertible roof. Barris also created a couple of process cars that were used for filming special stunts and effects. One was a convertible version which was towed behind the camera car.

While a major hit in the domestic television markets, *Knight Rider* was a popular program the world over. During its heyday, it was broadcast in almost every television market,

from England to Asia, including Germany, Japan, Spain, South Africa, Australia, and even the Middle East.

To satiate the frenzy created for related merchandise, Barris worked with model maker MPC to develop a one-twenty-fifth scale plastic kit of the versatile black beauty. Another deal was arranged with the Ertl/AMT company for the production of diecast, plastic, and tin toy versions of the fantastic *KITT* car. For Pontiac, the car—and the series—was a promotion better than any money could buy.

■

"Thanks to George for helping
to develop a car that has
a mind of its own. George really
is a legend in the car business."
David Hasselhoff

David Hasselhoff starred as Michael Knight in *Knight Rider*, a crime fighter equipped with a car that would put James Bond and his cars to shame. It could do virtually anything but sew on buttons.

Mannix

Television detective series ran from September 1967 to August 1975; Bruce Geller at DesiLu Studios, producer; CBS-TV. Starred: Mike Connors as Joe Mannix, Joseph Campanella as Lou Wickersham, Gail Fisher as Peggy Fair, and Robert Reed as Lieutenant Adam Tobias.

The *Mannix* television series had three notable points of interest: it was one of the most violent shows of the sixties, it was the longest running, and it featured a special George Barris custom Oldsmobile Toronado. Every episode featured at least one wild brawl and there were usually dead bodies sprawled out during the opening scenes of the program.

Joe Mannix was employed as a Los Angeles private detective by a sophisticated detective firm called Intertect. Lou Wickersham was Joe's boss and fellow investigator who used computers and other scientific methods to catch crooks. Mannix, however, was happiest working with his intuition and his fists. In the second season, Mannix went solo. Working as an independent, he had the help of his secretary and back-up crime fighter, Peggy Fair. Peggy's policeman husband was a friend of Mannix's who was killed in the line of duty.

For the series, Barris was asked to create an adventurous, sophisticated automobile that would suit a man of action. After looking over a series of

Mike Connors played Mannix for eight seasons. The Oldsmobile did great work, not only looking stylish and sophisticated but able to act as a high-speed pursuit vehicle.

The original illustration for the *Mannix Roadster* shows how well George's ideas flowed through into the final car. It was a nifty piece of design work that used the reliability of a production automobile and some stylish reworking to create a good looking, hard-working TV car that lasted eight seasons. This must be an industry record.

The *Mannix Roadster* is seen here on the set at the DesiLu Studios being prepared for a scene in an episode when Mannix goes back to the wild west. The camera crew, lighting technicians and general stage hands can be seen working on getting this scene ready to shoot. The full width custom rear end treatment of the Oldsmobile is quite apparent in this shot.

scripts, he decided that a convertible Oldsmobile Toronado would do the job. He presented his *Mannix Roadster* concept to producer Bruce Geller and series star Mike Connors, who both gave it their approval.

Barris transformed an Oldsmobile coupe into a roadster with a leather-covered tonneau cover installed over the rear seat area. This tonneau wrapped around the seats and formed a type of storage container for crime fighting and survival equipment. The interior also contained other amenities, including hidden gun compartments, radio-telephone, short-wave transceiver, and a tape recorder.

To create this Toronado *Roadster*, Barris fabricated a subframed X-member and installed it in the floor for strength. A sectional roll bar was also built which sat under the new tonneau cover. This new design followed much of what Oldsmobile had done with the Toronado's production bodywork. However, Barris created a clean, new look for the front and rear end of the vehicle by using many custom touches.

The nose was redone with new fenders, grille and lights. The fenders were extended and remolded with chrome caps on the tip. A new grille opening was fabricated and extended to blend in with the fenders. The grille was installed with a mesh backing topped with a fine tube grille and custom oval Cibie headlights. A special fiberglass hood was built with a pair of wind-splitter ridges that flowed back into the cowl.

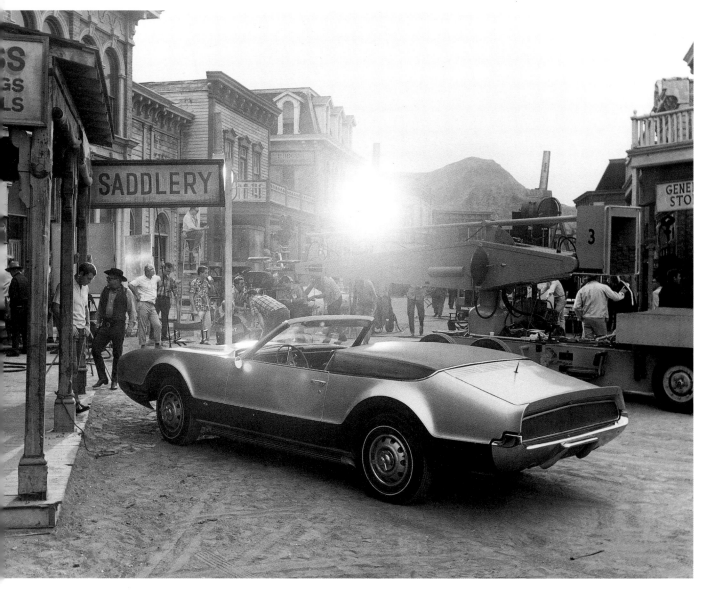

The *Mannix Roadster* was a large vehicle. Its redesigned rear end, two-tone body work and black leather tonneau all added to its character. Note how many crew members worked on the set preparing just one shot for the TV show! Only one actor is seen here, dressed in a cowboy outfit.

At the rear, Barris' design called for a spoiler that formed a recessed sequential taillight panel that used the stock bumper design. It was a neat custom trick. The trunk lid rolled down the bodywork and then rose up over the new spoiler—immediately falling away—much like a 1971 Pontiac Trans-Am. (Note: Barris designed the *Mannix* car in 1967). A set of side pipes was also installed and the roadster was painted platinum Star pearl metallic silver blue with black Star pearl on the lower quarter panels.

The convertible arrangement of Barris' concept proved perfect for filming. Because camera work was easier with an open car, the design presented more opportunities to see the star in action. As a result, the car appeared in many episodes of this popular television series. Its popularity was apparent since model toy maker MPC later released a one-twenty-fifth scale model of the Barris creation.

George is to the left of Mike Connors on the set of *Mannix*. According to George, Mike did many of the stunts in the show including some of the furious driving scenes using the Roadster. Mike liked the car's style and always enjoyed showing it off to interested visitors. The elegant front end treatment can be seen in this photo with its extended fenders, chrome mini-bumpers, custom chrome grille surround, and unusual headlight treatment.

The Silencers

Action/spy spoof movie in 1966; Phil Karlson, director; Columbia Pictures. Starred: Dean Martin, Stella Stevens, Victor Buono, and Daliah Lavi.

The *Silencers* was Dean Martin's first appearance as Matt Helm, the suave detective and ladies' man. Columbia Pictures produced this movie in an attempt to compete with the popular James Bond movies.

Matt Helm, the typical James Bond–type character, was a hip man-about-town. He owned a plush, four-door station wagon that just happened to turn into a mobile entertainment center. As would be expected from a playboy car, its rear compartment was built like a nightclub booth with curved padded seating, a bar, a wardrobe, and matching privacy curtains. Of course, the setup included a bed. Based on a 1965 Mercury Colony Park station wagon, the car was a central part of the movie as Matt Helm

moved about town chasing down the bad guys and seducing the ladies.

To meet the requirements for shooting, Barris was required to build three variations of the wagon given the name *De Elegance*. The first vehicle was a basic stunt wagon modified with a racing transmission, reinforced chassis, and heavy-duty wheels/tires. It was used for all the demanding driving scenes both on and off road as Helm was chased by the police and others.

Next came the "principal's car." Since the interior was to play an important part in the series, the wagon had to be designed so that cameras could shoot from different angles in the interior. The front seats were thinly framed buckets that could be turned backwards to face

Here George (right) confers with Bud Kunz and Les Tompkins over the blueprints for the wagons he was going to build for *The Silencers*. The film called for three versions of the same Mercury station wagon: a heavy-duty version for the driving and pursuit scenes, the principal's car which featured a complete custom interior, and a process car which featured a full custom interior but also broke down into sections so cameras could get the right angle.

The process car can be seen here in full operation. The camera crew and director Phil Karlson (coffee in hand), look on as Dean Martin and co-star Stella Stevens go through one of the nighttime driving scenes.

50

The heavy-duty stunt wagon was given a thrashing at times as this three-Ford scene with the Mercury wagon and two Ford Galaxies so dramatically shows.

the rear compartment. The central lounging area featured of an L-shaped sofa, curved and fitted with a fold-out cocktail bar, a gun compartment, and clothing storage. A second rear lounge was also built into the Mercury wagon. This space was filled with a U-shaped, padded sofa accessible from the tailgate (that folded down to form a step). This area could be sealed off for privacy with silk curtains and Venetian blinds.

Vehicle number three was what the film industry calls a "process," or breakaway body. While technically a simple build, it took hundreds of hours to assemble since it required a

complex structure to match the interior of the principal car, yet have the capability of being broken down into sections. Both the cowl and windshield section were removable so that cameras could face the actors, head on. This reinforced the illusion of driving. The car could also be halved across its middle and the cowl placed so that the cameras could shoot over the driver's shoulder. Other camera angles required removable door and roof sections.

This assembling and disassembling had to be done simply and quickly as the crew moved from scene to scene. Without a chassis, the body

was mounted on a steel jig framework with quick action couplers, using alignment pins that could be uncoupled in seconds.

The breakaway wagon's driving scenes for *The Silencers* were all filmed with a rear projection screen. Behind the stationary car, stock images of countryside, utility poles, and other street scenes rushed by. This technique (known in the biz as process filming) involves shooting the background location on both sides of the street or highway and then using close-up scenes with the actors inside the process car. Motionless, the car is mounted in front of the rear projection screen. When it's all put together, the illusion of driving down the road is a convincing one.

Another scene from *The Silencers* was a head-on crash between two Galaxies as the Mercury wagon swerved to miss the highway patrol car coming from the other direction. Both cars were built as break-away stunt cars with many parts set loosely into place so they would fly off on impact. The two crash cars were cut so they would split open on impact. Note the roof on the white Galaxie, and the doors and lights on the highway patrol car.

■

"I've always enjoyed the thrill of driving plus owning my many Barris Kustom Kars. It was like singing and dancing with fun."
Donald O'Connor

Chapter Three

Comedy on TV and in the Movies

The Beverly Hillbillies

Television situation comedy ran from September 1962 to September 1971; Paul Henning, producer; CBS. Movie in 1993; Penelope Spheeris, producer/director; Twentieth Century Fox Studios. TV series starred: Buddy Ebsen as Jed Clampett, Irene Ryan as Daisy Moses (Granny), Donna Douglas as Elly May Clampett, and Max Baer, Jr. as Jethro Bodine Clampett. Movie starred: Jim Varney as Jed, Cloris Leachman as Granny, Diedrich Bader as Jethro, and Lily Tomlin as Miss Jane.

This side view of the truck shows all the original body detailing with the original, old sign from the Fontana feed store still faintly visible. Also note the Non Skid tires, a rope holding the hood closed, and the glass-less headlights, all part of the Oldsmobile's detailing.

*T*he *Beverly Hillbillies* became one of CBS's longest running situation comedies. An irreverent look at life in Hollywood with the semi-slapstick Clampetts, it was based on the premise of an Ozark hillbilly family who had struck it rich with oil. After Jed accidentally discovered a massive holding of oil with a rifle shot, they were paid twenty-five million dollars from the OK Oil Company for drilling rights to their land. Eager to find a more refined environment (for children Jethro and Elly May), Jed moved the clan to "Cal-iforni" and into a Beverly Hills mansion.

This is perhaps the most famous photo of *the Beverly Hillbillies* from the first TV series. All the main characters, including the houn' dawg, are seen here cruising through Beverly Hills in the Oldsmobile as they arrive from the Ozarks. Both Jed and Granny have their hands clasped around shotguns and Jethro is doing the driving while Elly May is checking out the scenery.

Upon arrival, they deposited their newfound wealth in Milburn Drysdale's Commerce Bank. With his own agenda to look after the Clampett's money, Drysdale became their "guide" to living in Beverly Hills and had them purchase the huge mansion next to his so that he could help them "adjust." Mishaps and circumstances related to keeping their money in his bank became part of almost every episode.

George Barris was approached by series creator Paul Henning, who asked him to design a suitable vehicle. It was decided that a truck of some kind would be used to cart the family and their goods from the Ozarks to Beverly Hills.

Barris discovered the perfect starting point when he found a dilapidated, 1921 Oldsmobile touring car in the back of an old feed store in Fontana, California. He purchased the junker and immediately had it shipped back to his shop in

George was called upon to build this new hot-rodded Oldsmobile for the show in 1968. In one of the first shows of that season Jethro builds this hot rod from a mail order kit, then races Granny in the original truck. Granny beats him hands down after powering up her truck with "a good lickin' of white lightning racing fuel."

North Hollywood. He then set to work to create a driveable show vehicle.

The body had already been hacked off behind the front seat, so Barris created a platform with a park bench seat, about 30in higher than the front seat. Here, Granny and Elly May rode. Behind this cruise seat was space for hauling the family rocker, washtub, shotguns, and other family treasures. Interestingly enough, Barris didn't even have to paint the truck. The exterior finish had mostly disappeared, but the faded Fontana feed store sign was still visible on the side. This "original equipment" gave the Oldsmobile a wonderful personality—just right for the series.

In 1968, Barris was asked to create another ancient vehicle: an antique Olds truck hot-rodded by Jethro. Once again, he managed to scavenge up enough parts to create the look-a-like. Using a 1925 roadster found somewhere in Arizona, Barris rebuilt the wreck into a bright, candy apple red truck complete with yellow racing stripes, modified chassis, new brakes, and a custom interior. Under the hood was a 1969 442 Oldsmobile muscle car engine topped off with fake fuel-injected rams and

chrome sidepipes. A modern braking system and revised suspension were also installed, decked out with Cragar wheels and fat Firestone Indy Super Stock tires. The pickup bed was hand-built from wood to simulate the regular *Hillbillies'* truck. Twin parachutes were added for special effects.

In the program, the new hot rod made its debut when Jethro challenged Granny to a drag race. At the strip, Granny put the heat on Jethro after brewing up some special white lightning as racing fuel for her truck. Racing it backwards, she beat Jethro's crazy hot rod hands down—making this episode of the show one of the wackiest installments.

Eventually, both trucks were made into Model Products Company (MPC) 1/25th scale models. Other companies also took up toy licensing agreements for *The Beverly Hillbillies'* vehicles.

In 1993, Twentieth Century Fox Studios was planning to produce a new Beverly Hillbillies movie with a fresh set of actors, including Jim Varney as Jed, Lily Tomlin as Miss Jane, Cloris Leachman as Granny, and Diedrich Bader as Jethro. Once again, Barris was

For the new *Beverly Hillbillies* movie made in 1993 by Twentieth Century Fox Studios, George was contracted to recreate the original 1921 Oldsmobile Jalopy. It took some doing, but George located a body and radiator. He had to fabricate the rest of the car from scratch. This shot shows George in the driver's seat just after it came out of the shop. For the movie he still needed to decorate it with copies of all the original accessories, including the roped-down hood, old water barrels, broken garden rake, and kitchen utensils.

approached to create a "new" Jalopy truck. Since the original was now on display in an Ozarks museum, it was necessary to create a completely new vehicle for the movie. Somehow, Barris managed to find another 1921 Oldsmobile for the new project.

The new truck was built along the lines of the old truck but it utilized an all-new chassis underneath, fitted with a late model six-cylinder engine. An automatic transmission and hydraulic brakes were also added. The wheels used 23in vintage car tires but these were fitted to late model custom-made steel wheels with replica fiberglass caps that covered the entire wheel.

To match the patina of the original truck, the exterior of the new flivver was antiqued accordingly and fitted with an aging, hand-made bench for the comfort of back seat passengers.

The script for *The Beverly Hillbillies* movie also called for a second Clampett truck. In one movie scene, it was planned that a monster truck built by Jethro from the family truck be used to crush a row of expensive luxury cars. Utilizing an old racing monster truck once known as *Lethal Weapon*, George had Dick Dean create a Clampett behemoth with a replica of the Oldsmobile body. The monster truck that resulted was powered by a 528ci V-8 engine, was 25ft high, and weighed some 15,000lb.

A second Oldsmobile was also needed for the movie to replicate the hot rod version used in the TV series, but this time it was to be a monster truck hot rod. In the movie, Jethro builds the monster truck and then wreaks havoc in the country club parking lot. Stunt driver Jim Ries did "crushing work" in this scene with the monster Oldsmobile built out of the old *Lethal Weapon* racing monster truck.

The Flintstones

Comedy movie in 1994; Steven Spielberg, director (on movie poster listed as Steven Spielrock!); Hanna-Barbera/Amblin Entertainment. Starred: John Goodman, Rick Moranis, Elizabeth Perkins, Rosie O'Donnell, and Elizabeth Taylor.

In the original *Flintstones* cartoon, Fred Flintstone and his pal, Barney, spent a lot of time tooling around in their pedal-powered *Flintmobile*. Forget gasoline—when the time came to get moving, the stone-age pair simply dropped their legs through the floorspace opening and literally put their feet into it.

In 1994, a full-length feature film (carefully modeled after the classic animated series) hit the movie theaters. Comedy actor John Goodman played the ever-boisterous Fred and helped the film earn $37,000,000 during its weekend premiere—making it one of the top ten movie moneymakers of the year. George Barris Kustoms was once again an integral part of the equation.

For the movie version, Barris was asked to create a real-life facsimile of the cartoon Flintmobile. As happened, the contract called for not just one—

The *Flintmobiles* were kept simple as in the original cartoons. Here the wheel assemblies are being positioned before being installed on the main log bodywork. All the body pieces, including roof frames and the log wheels, were carved from foam before molds were taken and hard fiberglass parts made for use on the different Flintmobiles.

This electric-powered *Flintmobile* was built as a driveable process car that could be used in a simple way for action scenes without Fred or Barney having to overdo the foot-power and run out of breath. It sat a little higher than the basic foot-powered model but was fitted with side "logs" and filmed so the lower parts of the car were not seen.

The basic framework for the *Flintmobile* went together out of square and rectangular steel tubing. The framework was built and then reinforced before it was surrounded with its "wooden" bodywork. George is seen here with master fabricator Dick Dean assembling the first prehistory automobile.

The almost-completed *Flintmobile*—it just needs to be chased by a few saber-toothed tigers, dinosaurs, and other critters to get that "broken-in" look, and it'll be just perfect!

but several versions. A few were to be used as static models, while others were gas-powered process cars that were used for filming motion.

Barris created the prototype *Flintmobile* by carving out an idealized wood body from foam. Then, a set of molds were pulled from this master to make multiple fiberglass parts to be used in the additional vehicles. Simple steel frameworks were fabricated and became the chassis for the fiberglass log bodywork.

Some of the cartoon cars had rolling "log wheels," while others featured fixed rollers with small wheels hidden under them.

The process car was built from golf cart mechanicals attached to a custom-built steel frame. This allowed the actors to say their lines without exerting too much foot power to get the *Flintmobile* moving. In the area of bringing a cartoon to life, it was another success for Barris.

With its nicely wood-grained bodywork finished in earthy tones, saber-toothed tiger skin upholstery, and rock dashboard, the *Flintmobile* looked the part. After the movie the *Flintmobiles* went on a national and international promotional tour, appearing at movie premiers, toy stores, McDonalds restaurants, and auto shows.

The Good Guys

Television situation comedy ran from September 1968 to January 1970; Talent Associates, Inc., producer; CBS-TV. Starred: Bob Denver as Rufus Betterworth, Herb Edelman as Bert Gramus, Joyce Van Patten as Claudia Gramus, Ron Masak as Andy Gardner, Alan Hale, Jr., as Big Tom, Toni Gilman as Tom's girlfriend, and George Furth as Hal Dawson.

Actor Bob Denver was a hot television property during the late sixties. His runaway success with *Gilligan's Island* and *The Many Loves of Dobie Gillis* kept him in high demand. One of those demands became a new series called *The Good Guys*.

The main characters of *The Good Guys* were Rufus Betterworth and Bert Gramus, friends since childhood. Set in the city of Los Angeles, California, Gramus ran a diner called "Bert's Place" and was always involved in some sort of wild money-making scheme that never panned out. Rufus was a cab driver but gave up his taxi job at the start of the second season to become a full-time partner in the dining operation.

For the series, Barris was contracted to build a goofy taxi that Rufus would drive to earn a living. Based on a 1924 Lincoln Cabriolet Landaulet, it was designed as a special effects car. The doors could fall off if necessary or the headlights could be controlled remotely. Needless to say, Barris had a lot of fun building this television hot rod-taxi. Both of the rear doors were welded shut and the rear section of the body extended about 24in. The stock split windshield was retained but the original bumpers replaced. A modern nerf-style pushbar was up front, and the hood was modified with a pair of intake scoops.

Passengers entered the front passenger's side door and passed through a turnstile that activated a taxi meter. This meter was built from two Silex coffee pots bolted together at the mouth, one inverted. The joined pair acted like a giant hourglass, filled with Metalflake particles that poured down to create a metering system based on twenty-five cents per half mile. As extras, the taxi featured a triple set of horns, one from a Model T, a quad of air horns on the roof, and an Indian bulb horn. The

This shot on the set of *The Good Guys* shows the technical crew setting up the taxi with the anchor, as the film crew prepares to get rolling on the next scene, which was in front of the Out of Sight Go-Go Dancers' bar and disco. Note the various types of wheels fitted to the taxi and carried on the spare tire rack.

stretched rear section featured patched seat covers with just a few springs protruding, privacy shades, and a beach umbrella for the driver in case of rain. A doggie door, handrail (for picking up passengers from other moving vehicles), and slide-out extension step (for bridging the gap between the Lincoln's running board and curb) were also installed.

Barris equipped the Lincoln with a four-pronged reef anchor that was used to supplement the stopping power of the antiquated brakes. Many other neat things were added, including a hand brush in place of a windshield wiper, bright yellow paint, and a new black fold-

The Good Guys custom taxi was based on a 1924 Lincoln Cabriolet Landaulet. Bob Denver played Rufus, the driver of the taxi cab. The cab was designed with special effects: the doors could fall off if necessary and the headlights could be remotely controlled; it had an anchor if the brakes failed. This shot shows the three stars; left to right are Herb Edelman as Bert Gramus, Joyce Van Patten as Claudia Gramus, and Bob Denver as Rufus Betterworth.

ing top that featured porthole openings without windows. Large side and rear windows were fitted to make the camera work easier with the top in place. A set of wood-spoked alloy wheels went perfectly with the taxi's wacky character, amplified by the wicker trimmed side panels and rear double spare wheel rack.

Just after *The Good Guys* was introduced on the CBS network, MPC released a Barris special, Rufus Taxi kit. Today, this kit is considered a rare collector's item.

The Many Loves of Dobie Gillis

Television situation comedy ran from September 1959 to September 1963; Paramount. Starred: Dwayne Hickman as Dobie Gillis, Bob Denver as Maynard G. Krebs, Frank Faylen as Herbert T. Gillis, and Florida Friebus as Winifred Gillis.

The *Many Loves of Dobie Gillis* was one of America's favorite teenage television shows during the early sixties. The program lasted for four years and during that time, star Dwayne Hickman became the heartthrob of every teenage girl.

In the show, Hickman was cast as Dobie, a typical teenager interested in nothing more than beautiful girls, money, and fancy automobiles. As the son of an ordinary grocer, Dobie and his Beatnik pal Maynard did their best to get

According to George, the coupe was a big hit, especially with the star of the show, Dwayne Hickman, seen here with the coupe dressed and ready to do his show as Dobie Gillis.

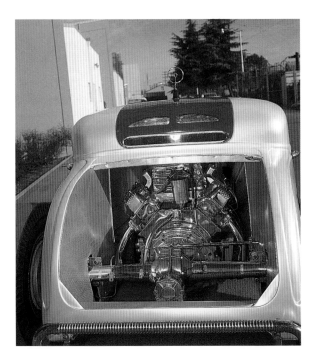

George set the coupe up as a street racer and had John Geraghty install a fully chromed blown Oldsmobile engine and rear-chromed suspension. Other changes included a chromed front suspension and a quick-change rear axle.

through their adolescence with a minimum of work and a maximum of fun. Two additional characters played off of this incorrigible duo: The intelligent (but unattractive) Zelda Gilroy and millionaire Chatsworth Osborne, Jr. Zelda's primary objective was to marry Dobie and Chatsworth's to simply flaunt his social status and money while pursuing the attractive girls who eluded Dobie.

Barris created a wild hot rod for the troupe. Like many deals in the movie business, the vehicle was once again needed within a very short time. Barris went on a hunting expedition and found that Art and Lloyd Chrisman's 1930 Model A Bonneville coupe was available. The Chrismans had built a gorgeous racer using a chopped 1930 Ford Model A coupe body and a pair of 1940 Ford hoods to form a streamlined nose. Back in the fifties, the coupe had run just over 196mph at the Bonneville Salt Flats. It was perfect for a quick makeover and use in *The Many Loves of Dobie Gillis*.

George changed the look of the Chrisman coupe with a new set of wheels. On the rear he installed a set of Halibrand Indy roadster-style magnesium alloy wheels, while up front he installed a set of chromed fuel-dragster spoked wheels. Aluminum wheel fairings added a dash of streamlining to the coupe. The body was reworked with half gull-wing doors so the car could be easily used for filming. The interior was fitted with aluminum panels and white pearl Naugahyde surfaces for the seats and door panels. The body was then repainted with thirty coats of a special Swedish pearl white lacquer that featured a diamond-like sparkle. To this were added candy tangerine panels on the roof and sides. For the show the coupe was renamed the *XMSC-210*.

The Munsters

Television situation comedy ran from September 1964 to September 1966; Kayro-Vue Productions, producer; Universal Studios. Starred: Fred Gwynne as Herman, Yvonne DeCarlo as Lily, Al Lewis as Grandpa Munster, Pat Priest as Marilyn, and Butch Patrick as Edward Wolfgang.

The Munsters were a "typical" American family who lived at 1313 Mockingbird Lane. But that's where any similarity with "typical" ended: even if it was sunny down the street, there was usually rain and winds howling around the Munster house. Their Gothic, cobweb-covered mansion looked just like the Addams family homestead. The head of the household was Herman, who was 7ft tall and bore a striking resemblance to Frankenstein's monster. The often befuddled Herman held a respectable job at the funeral home of Gateman, Goodbury & Graves but was always on the lookout for a way to make some easy money. His wife, Lily, dressed up in a gown that would be the envy of any lady vampire. Son Eddie was in the midst of an adolescent identity crisis as a wolf-boy who bayed at the full moon and slept with a werewolf doll called "Woof-Woof." Grandpa was a scary character too, a Count Dracula-type from Transylvania who had a

Parked outside, in front of 1313 Mockingbird Lane in Mockingbird Heights, the *Munster Koach* was an impressive vehicle from any angle. Close to 20ft long and 7ft high, it fit in perfectly with the run-down old house and its dead trees and overgrown yard. The fine detailing that the antiqued spiderweb-laced head-lamps, coffin handles, racing slicks, and a wild intake system on the engine.

This early shot of the *Munster Koach* shows the entire cast seated outside the sound stage at Universal Studios. The *Koach* had just been finished and George managed to get them all in his photo. Judging by their smiles they all liked their new ride. Herman and Grandpa are up front with Marilyn in the back seat and Lily and Edward Wolfgang Munster are on the footman's seat.

George had actress Pat Priest, who played Marilyn on the show, pose with the *Koach* for this Rader Wheel picture in front of his shop in North Hollywood. Decked out in a leopard skin print swimsuit with a perfectly coifed blonde hairdo, Pat looks like a picture postcard of a sixties Hollywood blonde bombshell.

lab in his dungeon and the ability to transform himself into a bat when the need arose. Herman's niece, Marilyn, lived with them and was considered the black sheep of the family. The Munsters thought her homely looking, but in fact, she was a Marilyn Monroe look-alike and the only "normal" member of the family.

The family pets included Spot, a stegosaurus found by Grandpa while digging in the back yard; Igor the bat; and a raven that popped out of a cuckoo clock to utter one annoying line of Poe: "Never more." In their house, books moved by themselves, breakfast

Drag-u-la was created for the second season of the Munster show. George designed this wild Ford-powered racing coffin for Grandpa Munster to drive and race, and the 289ci Mustang V-8 was built to show quality with plenty of chrome and color. The block was painted to match the purple coffin liner seat and the engine had been worked over with a dual quad manifold and high-compression pistons so it produced about 300hp. It is seen here with its first style of headlights. They were later changed to a pair of lights clad with spider webs and topped with metal spiders.

was cooked in a caldron, and when Herman blew a kiss, glass shattered.

Barris was brought into the series after the pilot created a surge of interest with the American viewing audience. Universal decided to go with a full season series and they figured an extraordinary-looking automobile would make a neat addition to the program. They looked for a suitably scary vehicle but couldn't locate one. Barris got the call and only three days to come up with a concept for the Munster family car.

With the help of his wife, Shirley, Barris put together visions of a long, hot-rod stagecoach, complete with a footman's seat, headstone-styled Model T radiator, red plush velvet upholstery, gas lanterns, curtained windows, coffin

The *Koach* and *Drag-u-la* can be seen match racing at the dragway. In typical Hollywood fashion a scene was created that wasn't true to life—all drag racing at this time used a Christmas Tree starting system and in this show a starter with a flag sent them off. *Drag-u-la's* wheels are 5in off the ground as it departs the start line with stuntman Jerry Summers at the wheel.

This picture was shot by George on the set of the TV episode when the *Munster Koach* and *Drag-u-la* went drag racing. It is interesting how much equipment and crew were needed to film this short segment of the show. Note the special lighting in the cabin of the *Koach* to light up Herman's face. Many single scenes needed to be shot to make this show work.

Other double car scenes in the TV show included a race between the *Koach* and *Drag-u-la* up a winding hill to the Munster's house. Here Grandpa outsprints the *Koach* with Herman at the wheel. This must have been a difficult scene to film at any sort of speed as the *Drag-u-la* was basically designed to run in a straight line, not go screaming around corners at high speed.

door handles, and antique lights with an eerie, spiderweb-motif. The *Munster Koach* was the result. The idea was a winner with Universal and Barris was given the immediate go-ahead to build the coach with the understanding that the job had to be complete in thirty days.

Barris set Les Tompkins and Bud Kunz to work building the *Koach* immediately. They fabricated a custom-built, hot rod-styled 133in wheelbase chassis, then made the six-door body from several fiberglass Model T bodies by stretching a 1927 touring car with an upright landau coach at center and a footman's seat in the rear.

The body was painted in gloss black pearl and was later spider webbed for a scarier appearance. Inside, the coach incorporated a portable chemical lab so that Grandpa could do

his experiments on the run. It was trimmed out with red diamond tufted velvet coffin liner with a Muntz eight-track stereo system, along with a pair of antique French telephones, and a Sony television receiver.

The *Munster Koach* rolled on a set of Ansen Astro wheels trimmed with knock-off hubs and walnut wood inserts, with a set of Mickey Thompson 11in wide slicks fitted to the rear wheels. A 289 Ford Cobra V-8 from a 1966 Mustang GT powered the coach. Barris had it built with Jahns high-compression pistons, a Mickey Thompson Long Ram manifold, ten chrome-plated Stromberg carburetors, an Isky cam, and a set of Bobby Barr racing headers. According to Herman Munster, "the *Koach* got three miles to each gallon of embalming fluid!"

Herman gives Grandpa safety advice at the wheel of *Drag-u-la* on the back lot at Universal. Note the Ford logo on the front of the car signifying that a 289 Ford V-8 was "laid to be restless" in the coffin.

Coming as no surprise, the *Munster Koach* was a real hit with viewers, evidenced by the large volume of fan mail received for the wagon by Universal. To satisfy the audience's desire to see it in action, they moved to incorporate it into more scenes on the show, including several episodes when it was raced. With its popularity, Universal also thought that a second Munster vehicle would make sense. Once again, they approached Barris and asked him to create something new for the second season.

A car for Grandpa was the result, a 160mph coffin on wheels dubbed *Drag-u-la*. Once again, Barris turned his imagination and crew loose to build the new car in a very short time. Using a Dragmaster chassis, a real coffin, and another 289 Ford, *Drag-u-la* was built quickly. Still, Barris

had a difficult time finding a real coffin because he wasn't in possession of a body or death certificate to go with it. Eventually, he managed to get a fiberglass coffin from a supplier and it was shipped back to the Kustom shop. The crew sliced the end off and then added 3ft so it would fit its new purpose.

Drag-u-la's chassis was set up with a single driving position behind the engine under a bubble canopy. A 350hp, 289 Ford Mustang V-8 with a four-speed stick, provided the motorvation. A pair of scoops diverted air into twin four-barrel carburetors and under the body. The hidden radiator was topped with a coffin-shaped header tank made of brass. A front-mounted Moon tank was used for fuel. George set the rolling stock in place with 11in Firestone drag slicks mounted on

Drag-u-la was a fully functional automobile that could be driven anywhere and was as much a hit with the cast as it was with the viewing public. The traffic on Riverside Drive in North Hollywood had a heck of a surprise when *Drag-u-la* went rolling by in the other direction during this photo session.

The Munsters went to England, taking along the *Koach* and *Drag-u-la* to make the movie *Munster, Go Home*. Herman raced *Drag-u-la* in a road race running up to 150mph and popping the parachute.

polished Rader five-spoke alloy wheels at the rear and English Speedsport wire wheels capped with Italian motorcycle tires up front.

The coffin bodywork featured a small grille to draw air into the radiator, gold-leaf paint finish, and a set of Huth "organ pipe" exhaust headers that sprouted from each side of the coffin. Barris finished off *Drag-u-la* with a miniature headstone set between the spider-webbed headlights and the front wheels. It read "Drag-u-la Born: 1367. Died - ?" Al Lewis, who played Grandpa Munster, summed up *Drag-u-la* in this way: "It's a dual purpose machine. You can go in it and you can *go* in it."

The car scenes in the series and movie *Munster, Go Home* were shot at the race

George recently built a second *Munster Koach* which was used in the new Munster TV special. He is seen here working in Dick Dean's shop with Keith Dean who helped in the fabrication of the new vehicle. The upright coachwork for the cabin was built with tubular steel framing and a plywood skin using a '27 touring tub at the rear with a hand-fabricated footman's seat made of scrolled steel.

track, drag strip, and on the street, using *Drag-u-la* and the *Munster Koach*. *The Munsters* became one of the most popular shows of the mid-sixties and both cars went on to achieve their own celebrity status. With shows that featured Grandpa hot footing it off the line at the drag strip with his front wheels flying and Herman giving a hapless driver's license examiner the ride of his life, Barris' monster machines entertained millions of people around the world.

In the 1980s, the *Munsters* enjoyed a comeback with a full-length movie called *Here Come the Munsters*. In addition, a one-hour television special was produced in 1995 called *Munsters Today*. The Barris *Munster* cars were highlighted in both programs.

My Mother the Car

Television situation comedy ran from September 1965 to September 1966; NBC-TV, producer. Starred: Jerry Van Dyke as Dave Crabtree, Ann Sothern was his mother's "voice," Maggie Pierce as Barbara Crabtree, Cindy Eilbacher as Cindy Crabtree, and Randy Whipple as Randy Crabtree.

In *My Mother the Car*, the affable Jerry Van Dyke played Dave Crabtree, a small-town lawyer who lived with his wife, two children, and a small dog. While searching for an inexpensive car at a used car lot, he finds himself attracted to a vintage 1928 Porter. When he gets behind the wheel, he hears something unexpected: a female voice coming from the radio. Who is it? It's his Mother reincarnated as a car!

The villain in the unusual car comedy is one Captain Bernard Mancini, a devious antique car collector who spends his waking hours trying to wrangle the Porter away from Dave. Episodes are spent in a variety of situations as Van Dyke fends off the interests of the relentless and unscrupulous collector.

Barris Kustom Industries built this matronly machine from various other vintage cars, including a Model T Ford, a Maxwell, a Hudson, and pieces from a Chevrolet. To make the vehicle appear driverless, the rear floorboard was cut out and a second driving position installed. As a result, the car could easily be driven by an experienced stunt driver using mirrors mounted underneath. The Porter was finished in Metalflake carnation red with a white top, and inside, buttoned upholstery in black.

Jerry Van Dyke is seen here on the lot at NBC Studios beside the Porter touring car. George had to build the Porter as a heavy-duty working machine, as it was expected to perform five days a week on the TV show. He powered it with a stock but reliable 283ci Chevrolet V-8 and a Powerglide automatic transmission, which made it easy to handle while filming and simple to maintain. The Porter was also exhibited in parades, mall displays, and at car shows around the nation. For exhibition purposes the car was equipped so it could talk to people at shows, let out whistles, and waggle its headlights.

The Van

Action/comedy movie in 1976; Paul Lewis, producer; Sam Grossman, director; Crown International. Starred: Stuart Getz, Deborah White, Harry Moses, Marcie Barkin, Bill Adler, Stephen Oliver, Connie Lisa Marie, and Danny DeVito.

The Van was one of those typical American exploitation movies. Central to the theme was a young man who gets the notion to forget about college and buy an expensive Dodge van. Figuring he can easily improve his social standing with this rolling bedroom-on-wheels, he cruises around the countryside in search of beautiful girls. Understandably, this Barris vehicle had a lot of competition from the bevy of babes wearing little more than short shorts. That's show business. Sometimes, even a classy car has to take the back seat!

Straight Arrow was one of many custom vans that the Barris shop built for this movie. Its "male symbol" graphics went hand in hand with the movie theme of the happy pursuit of beautiful girls.

■

"When it comes to performance, my Barris kustom car, *Travolta Fever* was a true 'Saturday Night Cruiser.'"
John Travolta

Chapter Four
Romance in the Movies

For Those Who Think Young

Movie in 1964; Essex Productions, producer; Leslie Martinson, director; Paramount. Starred: Nancy Sinatra, James Darren, Paul Lynde, Claudia Martin, Bob Denver, George Raft, Jack La Rue, Allen Jenkins, Woody Woodbury, Robert Armstrong, and Pamela Tiffin.

For Those Who Think Young revolved around a group of college kids who believed that surfing, music, and romance were grade subjects. With this in mind, their primary goal was to save the demise of their favorite club. While this age-old premise has been seen before, the movie did have a few distinctive features: Claudia Martin and Nancy Sinatra, the progeny of two famous stars, Dean Martin and Frank Sinatra. For car freaks, the attraction was more mechanical: George Barris' Buick *Villa Riviera* was also part of the show.

It all began when director Leslie Martinson was visiting the Barris shop to look over a vehicle that Barris Kustoms was building for another film. At the time, he was quite taken with the *Villa Riviera*, all decked out in cherry red paint

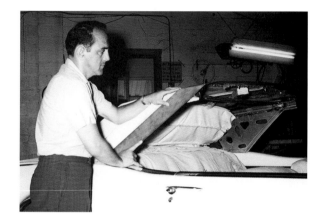

The *Villa Riviera* was built in North Hollywood and George is seen here examining how the new stainless molding fits over the edge of the newly chopped roof section. The landau roof was one of the most stylish sections of the car and fit perfectly with its restyling.

Using a 1963 Buick Riviera, George created the *Villa Riviera* Buick for himself. When it came time for the movie version, this illustration was done to show the Essex Production Company how the car would look. As it turned out, the car appeared quite different with its flying buttress roof and other custom body work.

The Buick was shot in many locations for the movie. Here we see James Darren and Bob Denver on the sound stage with the film and sound crew in place. Director Leslie Martinson is seated to the right as Darren and Denver ham it up in the Buick with its surfboards and twin dash-mounted telephones. The back projection shows the road behind the car for a road scene on the way to the beach.

over a fire frost white pearl base. Martinson quickly signed a contract that included a clause to repaint the Buick white so it would show up more clearly when filmed.

Originally, the *Villa Riviera* Buick was constructed as Barris' personal custom. He liked the look of the radically styled stock 1963 Buick

Riviera and began by sketching custom designs for a new version. His dominant criteria: create a sleek, semi-convertible, painted in cherry pearl red with a half landau white roof.

Buick supplied Barris with a new Riviera to modify and he began the project by completely reworking the front end—extending it 5in into a

On the set during an episode of the popular TV series *Perry Mason*. In this scene the Buick has been abandoned in a park after a chase and is being examined by police for fingerprints. The camera is mounted on a small powered dolly which is running on a board track in the lower right.

For *Those Who Think Young* was shot primarily on location with many outdoor scenes. The *Villa Riviera*, complete with a pair of Hansen surfboards, rolls by on Highway I and the truck-mounted camera catches the action as the Buick heads for the beach.

V-wedge design. The hood was ribbed, much like the deck on a sea-going power cruiser. Twin grille cavities gave the impression of a huge, scooped hood. The bumper in front was shaved off too, complementing the restyled sheet metal aprons that made up the new grille opening. Here, a center bar flowed up into the peak of the hood flanked by simple, vertical slats. For the existing hidden headlights, a fresh treatment of metal work made them appear even more prominent. All the trim and door handles were shaved and wheel openings radiused.

This rear shot, taken just after the Buick was finished in candy apple red, shows how well proportioned the coupe was with its new rear bodywork and cantilever white roof. At this time the Buick still sported a manufacturer's license plate.

This front view of the newly completed *Villa Riviera* shows how much work was done to the front end to change its appearance. From this angle it can be seen how the boat deck ribs on the hood matched the chromed vertical grille.

Astro air chrome reverse steel wheels were capped with tri-spoke, knock-off hubcaps.

Barris' modifications didn't end there. The rear end was reworked and stretched a full 5in. With the back bumper removed, the bodywork continued with the highpoint being a set of new taillights built into the mini tail fins. A new rear pan assembly was rolled into the body and the decklid incorporated a Frenched housing for the license plate.

The most significant change for the former Riviera was the landau-style cantilevered roof that gave the revamped version a semi-convertible look. This add-on half-roof was covered with Congo pearl white alligator hide edged with a brushed stainless steel band, capping the leading edge of the top. A two-section, T-top type cap was also made for the car which allowed the *Villa Riviera* to be quickly converted, at a whim, into a hardtop coupe.

The Buick went through several transitions including this silver-frosted paint scheme which highlighted the body molding and side panels. The Buick also featured cast aluminum wheels with two banded white wall tires. This paint scheme didn't last very long before the car was torn down and repainted in royal blue.

In the driver's compartment, trim was white leather all the way with walnut panels. An enhanced Autostereo sound system led the electronics package, one that included twin color-coded telephones and a removable Sony television set.

In the motion-picture, the *Villa Riviera* was used for all kinds of activities, including chasing girls, cruising, and hauling surfboards to the beach.

The car also appeared in several television shows, including *Perry Mason*, and toured the show car circuit. Its most notable achievement was being named "Movie Car of the Year" in *Hot Rod* magazine's Custom Car Yearbook Number Two. Since the sixties, the *Villa Riviera* has changed owners, and colors, several times. Most recently, it has been beautifully restored in dark blue by its current owner, Bill Ryan.

High School Confidential

*Movie in 1958; Jack Arnold, director; MGM. Re-titled and reissued twice: first as Young Hellions, then as College Confidential.
Starred: Russ Tamblyn, Mamie Van Doren, John Barrymore, Jackie Coogan, Charles Chaplin, Jr.,
Lyle Talbot, Michael Landon, William Wellman, and Jan Sterling.*

High School Confidential was the typical American car/teenager movie featuring a rowdy group of high school kids who got their kicks necking at the drive-in, dragging down Main Street, and playing chicken on the outskirts of town. In the flick, Russ Tamblyn played a rookie undercover cop bent on busting the local marijuana smokers and drug pushers, who just happen to be hot-rodders. As the movie proceeds, Tamblyn keeps it lively with plenty of jive talk and high-octane action—including street races and crashes set against a pulsing soundtrack of Jerry Lee Lewis rock and roll.

Interestingly this motion picture was one of the first Hollywood movies to feature hot rods and customs to be constructed specifically for a motion picture. To create the vehicles, the Barris Brothers took two 1948 Chevrolet coupes and reworked them with chopped tops, tear drop skirts, custom grilles, blanked out side windows, and lowered suspensions.

According to George, "Sam and I installed a roll cage in one of the Chevys because it was to be rolled in a scene. However, the stuntman, Gary Laufer, couldn't roll it because it was too low. He tried a half dozen passes but there was no way he could get it over. So, they simulated the rollover by dropping the Chevy from a crane which made the wheels fly off and the doors pop open."

The movie business introduced hot rods and custom cars into their productions in the late forties. *High School Confidential* was one of the first to feature hot rods and customs built specifically for a movie when they filmed it in 1957–58. The Barris brothers built two 1948 Chevys with teardrop skirts, custom grilles, blanked out side windows, lowered suspension and chopped tops. Sam Barris had already chopped the top and filled in the quarter windows of one Chevy in this photo. The other car is still unmodified.

Here the Chevy in *High School Confidential* pursues a couple of roadsters in the street races just before the rollover scene. Barris installed a roll cage in both Chevys for safety, but Gary Laufer, the stuntman, couldn't roll it because of its low stance. The scene had dozens of spectators cheering the illegal racing activities before the big crash.

One of the custom Chevy coupes survived the movie and was restored some years later by the Barris shop. The roll bar can still be seen as well as the chopped top, Frenched headlights, and unique custom grille.

■

"My Rolls-Royce would not be royalty,
unless coachbuilt by you, George Barris."
Zsa Zsa Gabor

Marriage on the Rocks

Romance/comedy movie in 1965; Jack Donohue, director; Warner Brothers. Starred: Dean Martin, Deborah Kerr, Frank Sinatra, Cesar Romero, Hermione Baddeley, Tony Bill, Nancy Sinatra, John McGiver, and Trini Lopez.

This wacky, romantic love triangle starred Deborah Kerr, Dean Martin, and Frank Sinatra. In the movie, Deborah and "old blue eyes" are married and have a falling out. They get a quickie divorce in Mexico, leaving them free to pursue other interests. Kerr promptly marries Martin.

George Barris was requested to come up with a couple of special cars for this movie and produced two winners. The first was a totally wild, Ford Mustang custom—an obvious choice since Barris figured he could restyle it radically to produce an interesting, futuristic custom. To achieve this, he took a stock Mustang and converted the hardtop to a Targa roof, just like the one he had on the *Villa Riviera* Buick used in *For Those Who Think Young*.

The profile was revamped with a new front end treatment that resulted in a fully customized *Zebra Mustang* that was not readily identifiable as a 1965 Mustang. Barris clipped off the nose and replaced it with a handformed metal grille that featured a huge oval opening. This scheme

The building of the *Zebra Mustang* was no simple custom project. All the sheet metal was changed, as you can see in this photo. The sheet metal for the new front end was extended over 10in and was handformed and gas-welded in 20-gauge steel. Here, George confers with Richard Korkes, his project engineer, over the placement and installation of the four French Cibie headlights.

This photo from the set of *Marriage on the Rocks* once again shows how large a crew of people it took to make a movie—and this shot does not show the whole crew. The *Zebra Mustang* is parked in a driveway for this scene and from this angle you can see how much work went into the restyling of the rear end GT-look and the new roof. The taillight was a double full width unit separated by a narrowed slice of bodywork.

worked well with deeply Frenched, oval head-lights and a hood that was stretched 4in. A seven rib, aluminum flat bar-stock grille was formed into a "V" shape to complete the new front end.

The rear end treatment was just as extensive. All the original sheet metal was replaced with new handformed components. The rear end work started out with the cantilever Targa roof section which rolled back from above the front seats and sloped down to the end of the trunk lid. A full-width taillight was fabricated, along with a new rolled rear panel, Frenched license plate holder, and extended fender tips that formed a neat pair of pointed tail fins.

Just as dramatically, side panel contours were changed. Both of the wheel wells were given molded body lines that flowed from the tip of the fender (along the top of the reshaped wheel opening) and formed a flared lip. At the rear, this shape was duplicated, running around the front of the wheel opening to form a matching fender flare, then trailing to meet the apex of the new fenders.

For the exterior, the *Zebra Mustang* was painted in a two-tone motif. Pearl white made up the main body color with black on the trunk lid and Targa roof. Fade-aways done in pearl red highlighted the under edge of the new body lines. The original coved side panels were removed along with the door handles. These side panels were covered with faux "baby" Zebra skin (patterned fabric) and leather accents, surrounded by chrome trim. The roof was also wrapped in

Here George is with Frank Sinatra on the movie set on the day he delivered the car. This angle shows how deeply the headlights were recessed into the tunnels that formed the front end.

the same imitation skin, complementing the four similarly covered custom bucket seats inside. A carpet of black Mouton fur topped it all off and took the animal theme to the extreme.

The second vehicle Barris made for this movie, to be driven by Dean Martin, was a custom 1966 Thunderbird convertible. The Ford Company shipped the Thunderbird to the Barris Kustom shop in early 1965, months ahead of its introduction, so that Barris could finish all the modifications and Warner Brothers would have enough time to shoot before the car officially debuted as Ford's latest model. (Note: The 1995 James Bond production *Goldeneye* also used a new auto prior to its scheduled public release; however, the new BMW Z-3 Sports Roadster was not modified).

To make it unique, the Thunderbird received a full custom rear end treatment, shaved body, custom two-tone paint, and a roadster tonneau

cover. The front end was completely reworked, although it still retained the basic side profile. According to Barris, Dean Martin himself approved the restyling on the Thunderbird and even suggested a few changes of his own as the work progressed. Still, Barris came up with most of the innovations, including a rear end rework that featured twin Frenched custom taillights with ribbed aluminum trims that covered the new taillights. The Thunderbird was eventually repainted in a striking platinum starflake with side panels fading into strawberry candy red.

In the movie, Nancy Sinatra drove the Mustang in numerous scenes while Dean Martin drove the Thunderbird. As history and reviewers have made obvious, the two late model customs were more memorable than the motion picture itself. Both of these Barris cars are now in a private collection in Anaheim, California.

This 1965 Thunderbird was the second custom that George built for the movie. This gorgeous T-bird featured all the usual custom touches including shaved trim, custom taillights, and rear end treatment. The front end was reworked with an extended hood, three-element grille design with twin peaks and custom ribbed grilles, and a pair of French oval Cibie headlights from a Renault. The paint was also wildly customed, featuring Platinum Starflake with a side panel fadeaway of strawberry candy red that matched the Thunderbird's red interior.

Super Van

Action/romance movie in 1977; Sal Capra, producer; Lamar Card, director. Starred: Katie Saylor, Mark Schneider, Morgan Woodward, and George Barris.

SuperVan was a double header for George Barris. Not only did he build the vehicle that was the central theme of this movie, but he also appeared as the *SuperVan's* creator and "King of the Kustomizers." The van was portrayed as a high-tech, solar-powered, futuristic vehicle that without a need for gas, could solve the world's oil shortage problem. For most of the film, the "competition" tries to steal it. Barris built the vehicle for use on the show car circuit at the height of America's van craze. When the concept for the movie came along, the van was a perfect, and readily available, choice for the job.

Poster for *SuperVan*

Built on a Dodge Sportsman Van chassis, the SuperVan incorporated a low beltline into its almost symmetrical futuristic styling. The van, powered by a 318 Chrysler V-8, featured Charcoal-tinted Polaroid glass, a gullwing side door, and a body painted in burnt orange and bright sky blue candy. A set of solar panels flipped out of the roof so they could be angled to follow the sun and the interior was set up as a luxurious living and entertainment center. Seen here on the set, the *SuperVan* is positioned on a slippery hill during filming.

Chapter Five

Musical and Youth TV Shows and Movies

The Bugaloos

TV series for 1970–71 season; Krofft Productions, producer; NBC-TV. Starred: Martha Ray, Caroline Ellis, John Pilpot, John McIndoe, and Wayne Laryea.

The *Bugaloos* buggy was another television show car constructed especially at the Barris Kustom shop for Krofft Productions. The producers desired a small, wild-looking, fun buggy to incorporate into their new NBC-TV series, *The Bugaloos*.

Set on a Utopian island called Tranquillity, *The Bugaloos* was primarily a comedy-fantasy program that featured four teenage musicians and a "rock witch." The four main characters were a do-good musical group who dedicated their lives to helping those in need. They possessed wings and wore outfits that resembled butterflies, bees, and other insects. Their arch rival was Benita Bizarre, the rock-and-roll witch who lived in a noisy jukebox.

Martha Ray starred as Benita Bizarre, who held court over an eclectic cast of characters—including Funky Bat, Peter Platter, and the Stereo Twins: Woofer and Tweeter. The main premise of the show revolved around the witch, who threatened the harmony of the Bugaloos and their efforts to do good (and play music at the same time) in show after show.

To supply an automotive interest for the series, Barris built the a buggy in late 1969 to be used in the 1970–71 TV season. His motivation: the vehicle was to possess all of the fun characteristics that made the Meyers Manx dune buggy famous—yet push the concept beyond the envelope with attention-getting color and design elements. The goal was a completely different and vibrant look.

Using a four-passenger body mounted on a Volkswagen floorpan, the buggy actually looked just like a bug—mixing well with the show character who could fly and walk on water like little flying insects. The design featured a T-shaped rollbar set over the rear wheels with a pair of "wings" that gave the effect of an airborne bug yet allowed plenty of space for television camera maneuvers. The chassis rolled on Ansen Sprint alloy wheels, highlighted with orange spoked centers. The fully fendered four-wheeler featured oversized headlights that looked just like bug eyes. On the outside, the paint scheme was a wild combination of green, yellow, and orange, applied to copy the markings found on a butterfly's wing.

There was much more. The interior was fitted with four custom bucket seats with leaf-like design elements that continued the buggy's nature theme. Four Capitol Communications telephones and four Muntz stereo tape cartridge players were also installed. A four-tone horn was on board as well, offering a distinct tone for each one of the characters.

Fully street legal, *The Bugaloos* buggy was used extensively in the show. When the series was introduced to the airwaves, Barris contracted with model kit manufacturer MPC to design a plastic model kit based on the program vehicle.

The finished buggy looked just like its original design. George was mindful of the need to have the vehicle as flexible as possible for camera use and built it with a wide open cabin so that the characters could be easily lighted and filmed. Seen here on the set for the show, the buggy's winged styling was perfect for its insectoid characters and its paintwork was trendy for the late sixties, mixing the details found on butterfly wings with psychedelic shapes. There was another buggy in the show known as the *Baroque Buggy* that Benita Bizarre drove. She kept Peter Platter, the Uptown disc jockey from radio station KOOK, spinning the hard rock while the Bugaloos fought back with soft rock and sweet harmonizing.

Easy Come, Easy Go

Action/musical movie in 1967; Hal Wallis, producer; John Rich, director; Paramount Pictures. Starred: Elvis Presley, Dodie Marshall, Skip Ward, Frank McHugh, Pat Priest, Pat Harrington, and Elsa Lanchester.

In the movie *Easy Come, Easy Go,* hip-gyrating singer Elvis Presley played a Navy frogman who dives for underwater treasure. This light-hearted romp was complete with musical numbers, beach scenes, beautiful girls, and fast cars. This is a typical "Elvis movie," a format popularized during the 1960s. This movie, of course, includes an ample dose of singing (though none of it underwater), a little romance, and time spent in a racy roadster. A *Mongrel T* hot rod touring car built by Barris is the ride of choice for the "Hound Dog" crooner.

Seen here on the beach during filming, the *Mongrel T* used a mix of parts with a custom-built extended '27 Ford touring car body featuring a Rolls-Royce radiator, antique brass headlights, a 289 Ford V-8 powertrain, and Radar alloy wheels.

92

The lengthened bodywork included fabric-covered doors and wood panels while the interior featured multicolored Icelandic sheepskins and four-place seating complete with Hansen surfboards as backrests.

With Elvis in this still is one of the many beauties of the film, along with Pat Harrington in the back seat.

■

"Thanks for the memories of the great times I had with the klassic kart you kustomized for me."
Bob Hope

Good Times

Romance/musical/comedy movie in 1967; Lindsley Parsley, producer; William Friedkin, director.
Starred: Sonny and Cher, George Sanders, Norman Alden, and Larry Duran.

nitially, the Sonny and Cher Mustang project called for only one car—but the reality of trying to mix both male and female ideas into one vehicle soon had two Mustangs being built. One was made for Sonny, the other for Cher. Both custom Mustangs had a double purpose: they were to be personal cars for the singers and would be used in the movie *Good Times*.

This was the first production directed by William Friedkin and featured Sonny and Cher playing themselves. The premise was two hopefuls acting out a fantasy to become movie stars and singers, with notable hits such as "I've Got You Babe" performed in the process. In this melodic movie, the Barris Mustangs are driven around Hollywood and the motion picture studios.

The exterior design of both Mustangs were identical, with new grille openings, oval headlamps, custom hoods, and rear end treatments. Customizing work extended to creating a new double cavity grille

George and Sonny pick fabrics while Shirley Barris and Cher discuss floor coverings. Cher is holding some samples of the 3in long Mouton fur carpet which was eventually fitted to both vehicles. Sonny has his arm over a concept view of the Mustangs.

opening—with reverse center nose appendages that cut back into the hood center. A pair of oval-shaped French Cibie headlamps were installed that had large chrome escutcheons and matching double cavities. A new rear end treatment matched the front to rear end, with grilles over the new Frenched taillights. Other body modifications included shaved door handles,

Sonny and Cher were keen to see the custom Mustangs on the road and came by the shop each week to see the progress. With the Mustangs about half done, some of the extensive bodywork changes can be seen here including the oval headlight opening, flared wheel arch and the new fender profile welded.

The Mustangs were used in the filming of *Good Times*, Sonny and Cher's first movie. In this scene, with a child playing a cowboy, you can see how George re-did the side of the convertible without door handles and custom trimmed the covered side panel with a deeper two-tone paint scheme. Sonny's Mustang can be seen parked off screen while filming continued into the evening. The lighting crew look on as the camera crew go through the motions of getting another take in the can.

radiused wheel openings, and 2in flares. The power-plants were also the same, each featuring a 289 Mustang motor retrofitted with twin, four-barrel carburetion and chrome dress-up kits.

However, the Ford ponies were really only paternal twins. Sonny's sportster featured an egg-crate grille in the front and rear, along with hood scoops. It was painted in murano gold pearl with brown side panels and fade-away orange/gold tonings over the wheel wells and around the grille openings. Inside, it featured a horseshoe motif, with Bobcat fur and antique buff leather trimmed in rustic suede. Even more exotic was the unusual floor covering comprised of 3in-long, gold Mouton fur.

In contrast, Cher's personal Mustang featured ribbed grilles and a different style of Rader wheels. It was an eye-catching convertible that featured an exterior of hot pink pearl blended with candy red, deep red side panels, and matching fade-aways over the wheels and around the front and rear grilles. Her driving compartment

Sonny's Mustang matched Cher's except for the body color, the wheel style, grilles and the interior trimming. All the wheel wells were radiused and flared with the paint blended over each opening. The body color was done in Murano Gold Pearl with brown side panels and featured fade-away orange/gold tonings. The egg crate grille can be clearly seen on the car from this angle. It differed from Cher's, which had cross textured grilles.

featured white ermine and black antique Scottish grain leather trimmed in hot pink suede. Matching floor covering was 3in-long, hot pink Mouton fur.

As often happens with promotional movie vehicles, Sonny and Cher didn't really get to drive their Mustangs very often. Almost immediately upon completion of the movie, the automobiles were taken on a national tour of shopping malls, auto shows, and other promotional events. Once this promotional tour was over, both cars were returned to Sonny and Cher, who then used them regularly.

The AMT Corporation made a double "His and Hers" one-fourth scale plastic kit of the Sonny and Cher Mustangs that allowed either of the two versions to be assembled. Today, this model is a highly collectable kit. After all, the interest in these unique, custom Mustangs still exists. Recently, they were proudly exhibited at a Goodguys West Coast hot rod show.

Groovy

Teenage TV series. KHJ-TV-9 in Los Angeles, producer. Starred: Mike Blodgett.

Groovy was California beach music show in the pre-MTV days of the sixties. This teenage romp of sea and surf featured plenty of action with music and dancing on the beach. Filmed in Santa Monica, California, it starred Mike Blodgett as host and was the predecessor of today's beach-based top forty shows.

Barris built a pair of Sand Chariot dune buggies for this production, one finished in bronze red metallic paint complete with a flowered pattern roof (talk about flower-power) and inside matching upholstery. The second buggy got its own dose of the psychedelic treatment: it was completely covered in flower decals.

The first vehicle was dubbed the *Groovy Ocelot* and was driven right there on the beach. Later, it was made into a one-twenty-fifth scale model by model-making concern MPC.

The *Groovy Ocelot* buggy was used for *Groovy* show promotions around Los Angeles at shopping malls, car shows, and in parades. The *Sand Chariot* buggy was built with a flowered convertible top, an idea started by the originator of the dune buggy, Bruce Meyers.

George chats with Mike Blodgett on the set of *Groovy*. Mike is seated in the *Groovy Ocelot* buggy fitted with its huge Goodyear Extra Trac sand tires, stinger exhaust, and Cragar alloy wheels. George appeared on the show demonstrating how much fun these buggies could be on the sand.

Out of Sight

Spy spoof/comedy/musical movie in 1967; Bart Patton, producer; Lennie Weinrib, director; Universal Studios. Starred: Jonathan Daly as Homer, with Karen Jensen, Billy Curtis, Rena Horton, Bob Pine, Norm Grabowski, Carole Shelayne, Gary Lewis and the Playboys, The Turtles, Dobie Gray, and Freddie and the Dreamers.

Out of Sight was a spoof of the highly popular James Bond spy movies. At the same time, it had all the essence of a good comedy: a butler played by Jonathan Daly and a crazy blonde played by Karen Jensen became involved in a plan to stop a secret spy organization called FLUSH. The outfit is a conspiracy against rock groups! This combination rock-and-roll spy spoof and beach-party movie included great performances from the popular bands Freddie and the Dreamers, Gary Lewis and the Playboys, and The Turtles.

During preproduction, the studio contacted Barris to secure a suitable vehicle for the movie. They wanted something that was not only wild—but wacky. And they wanted it immediately. Unfortunately, Barris had nothing on hand that was weird enough and as a result, created a wild

twin-engined hot rod along the lines of the *Munster Koach*. With the standard four-week deadline agreed to, Barris commissioned Les Tompkins to begin work on a 135in chassis built in a box section tube with a pair of Buick V-8 engines hooked up in line.

A simple dropped tube solid axle was used up front, with split radius rods while a coil/over rear suspension was created on an Oldsmobile axle at the rear. A Ford Econoline steering box was installed with an extra long drag link to the front end. The 304ci engines were hooked up with a dog-clutch arrangement built by Tompkins so they could be operated either as a pair or using only the rear engine. A single, two-speed, Ansen Posi-shift Powerglide transmission moved the horses down to the rear wheels.

Jonathan Daly starred as Homer the butler who somehow manages to get Karen Jensen involved with fighting a conspiracy against rock and roll. Homer gets his hands on the *ZZR* hot rod and they head to the beach for surfing, music, and party times, fighting off FLUSH along the way. The *ZZR* featured two Buick V-8 engines and enough weird stuff to drive any spy crazy. Homer appears to be asking Karen to gently remove herself from his number two engine.

George built this sidecar-equipped Yamaha 250cc *Big Bear Scrambler* motorcycle for the movie using a Cal Automotive fiberglass 1915 Model T car body. The sidecar was formed by shortening, narrowing, and shaping the body into a V to create a suitable chase vehicle for FLUSH organization members by Rena Horton and Billy Curtis. Note the mortar tube mounted on the side.

The body was constructed around a Cal Automotive fiberglass 1927 T Touring body with extended doors and a custom-made roof. The rest of the body was entirely hand fabricated.

The body was channeled down over the frame and a tall double-glass windshield built to make the cabin stock height. Tilted forward, the rear section gave the car a jauntier look as did the padded roof, complete with portholes. The fenders were another interesting creation: At the rear, they used a set of modified 1927 T fenders but in the front, the fenders were done with long, flying low V-panels that started out in front of the doors and stretched forward through a side-mounted spare wheel and on out over the front wheels, past the dual Buick powerplants.

A unique front end was created with a giant, floating brass radiator cupped into the bodywork. A pair of rectangular headlights were mounted vertically surrounding the radiator. Dual Italian air horns played the program's theme song.

The *ZZR* hot rod was equipped with assorted spy spoof equipment. The interior even had a "Press to Smell" button that when pressed, squirted the presser with sleeping gas! The *ZZR's* weapons cache was just as strange, featuring a tar and feather shooter, a trick passenger seat that flopped forward to knock all unwanted passengers unconscious, and an arsenal of assorted weapons. Machine guns were mounted in the tips of the front fenders and a parachute at the rear to engulf pursuing vehicles. A flame thrower exhaust, rocket launchers, and an oil slick spreader came standard. There was even a set of antique Italian rear vision mirrors that could punch a bad guy on the chin.

None of the above were EPA, DOT, or even CHP approved, but for a teenage spy-spoof movie, they all met with rousing approval. The *ZZR* was, in theory, also able to convert itself into a roadside billboard as camouflage from pursuing secret agents. This was done with movie effects rather than with a mechanical adaptation.

The rod was finished in Golden Fleece gold flake lacquer with two-toned ultraviolet flake

The *ZZR* started out with a custom rectangular tube chassis, Oldsmobile rear axle, and a solid dropped front axle. Having already built an extra long rod for the *Munsters*, George comfortably went to work on the *ZZR*. George (right) is seen here with Tex Collins as the rod went together. The first engine is in place but there was other chassis engineering to be done including a steel truss to reinforce the frame. One of the major tasks of doing a job like this, according to George, is making sure all the prefitted pieces work with the next part to be installed. The body was a Cal Automotive '27 T touring tub but George used it in his own way with a high rake on the rear and a low set cowl channeled down over the chassis. Les Tompkins mated a pair of 304ci Buick engines using a custom dog-clutch arrangement so the engines could be operated as a pair or by using only the rear engine. A single two-speed Ansen Posi-shift Powerglide transmission was attached to the rear Buick.

At the rear of the *ZZR* George installed a super weapons compartment with a variety of guns, bombs, and smoke devices. A parachute was installed above the weapons compartment.

fenders. Padded gold Naugahyde trimmed the top, with the doors and side-mounted spare wheels capped with a padded center section to match.

Barris also produced a customized Yamaha motorcycle equipped with a T-touring car bodied sidecar for this rock musical. This was used by midget actor Billy Curtis and starlet Rena Horton who were the bad guys pursuing the *ZZR* hot rod. Some of the scenes were filmed on location in Malibu at a custom beach pad.

Model maker AMT became interested in the *ZZR* rod and produced a one-twenty-fifth scale model of the *ZZR* spy rod from *Out of Sight* just after the movie was released. In 1996, the car made a reappearance: Playing Mantis released a one-forty-second scale model of the *ZZR* in its Johnny Lightning Series.

Romp

Television musical comedy special in 1968; NBC-TV, producer. Starred: Jimmy Durante, Liberace, Michelle Lee, Michael Blodgett, and Ryan O'Neal.

Romp featured famous musical performers and a collection of special vehicles. George Barris built three cars for the show: a modified GTO, a motor coach, and a Pontiac Firebird convertible.

The motor coach was constructed as a huge recreational center and styled like a Chris Craft motorboat. It featured polished wood paneling and huge musical notes. The driver's position was mounted on the roof in a flying bridge, with a boat windshield and railings around the edge.

It came ready-equipped for sports and fun, with surfboards clipped to the sides, a lifeguard tower, huge jukebox, an aqua-slide, a tag-along power boat, and pair of Yamaha motorcycles mounted on a side rack. On the show, it toted musical equipment and was home to a group of traveling female vocalists.

The first of two high-performance Pontiacs that Barris built for the show was just as amazing. It was a GTO hardtop that was modified to

The motor coach, or rather, land yacht, from *Romp* is seen here overflowing with young ladies. The twin steering flying bridge can be seen on top, with its lifeguard tower and boat railing. A diving board is also mounted off the rear and the jukebox and surfboards are ready for fun. The land yacht also towed an inboard power boat for water skiing.

look like a cartoon police car complete with graphics, external roll bars, and lights. Its body was sprayed with wild black-and-white patterns. Air horns and ram tubes were mounted on the hood. Side pipes were part of the package, as was a huge gold police star emblazoned on the door. It was referred to as the *Fuzz Car* and Jimmy Durante played the policeman who drove it.

The second Pontiac was a 1967 Firebird convertible. It was repainted with a flower and music motif especially for a song called "Daisy Fields," sung by the group The Celebration. With its bold graphics and splashy colors, it carried the band onto the set prior to their performance on the program.

The *Fuzz Car* was built from a '69 GTO. It featured a wild black-and-white paint scheme and a full collection of police accessories plus twin external roll bars. In the show, the car was used by actor Jimmy Durante who played "The Fuzz." A young Ryan O'Neil is seen here with Jimmy Durante.

On the set of the TV special the performers, including the group The Celebration, are ready for action. The Firebird was painted as a kind of flower-power, hippie convertible. Words from the song "Daisy Fields" were painted on the body along with the music and the flowers. There were many girls in miniskirts, singing, dancing, or riding motorcycles.

Village of the Giants

Science fiction/fantasy movie in 1965; Berkeley Inc. Productions, producer; Bert I. Gordon, director. Starred: Tommy Kirk, Ronny Howard, Johnny Crawford, Beau Bridges, Tim Rooney, and Joy Hamon.

Village of the Giants was based on an H. G. Wells science fiction story about a town where a group of kids find a transforming liquid. After drinking some, they discover that it changes them instantly into 30ft giants! As they grow accustomed to this unnatural growth spurt, they descend upon the town and begin wreaking all sorts of havoc.

Part of this destruction includes another Barris vehicle. It was a Hemi-powered, 1927 hot-rod roadster that didn't need the body to function. Key to the design (and the special effects) was a spring-loaded body that was hinged at the rear end. When one of the unruly giants stepped on it, the body flipped up and appeared to fall apart.

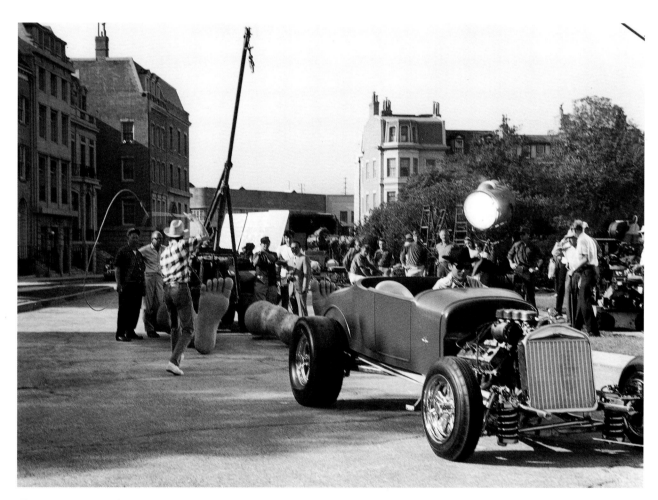

The Barris shop built this highly detailed '27 roadster featuring a chromed chassis and a Dodge Hemi V-8 with four carburetors and Rader alloy wheels. George helped supervise the stunts during the making of the film; in this scene everything worked out just as planned, with the body flipping off as the giant teenager stepped on the rear of the car. The '27 T roadster is seen here as it is pulled away just before the body is flipped off.

The '27 roadster which George custom-built for *Village of the Giants* is seen here outside the Barris workshops in North Hollywood. He designed it with a fully chromed chassis, a coil spring-suspended tube axle, a Hemi V-8, and Rader alloy wheels. The body was designed to flip up off the chassis using a spring loaded pivot at the rear of the chassis. From this photo you can see how the body and chassis easily separated.

Chapter Six
Car and Hot Rod Movies

Hot Rod Gang

Teenage drama/action movie in 1958. Lew Landers, director; Allied Motion Pictures. Starred:
Gene Vincent, Jody Fair, John Ashley, and Steve Drexel.

This teenage hot-rod movie was a classic reel of gasoline-powered action portraying the trials and tribulations of American youth in pursuit of automotive dreams. The premise: a youngster from the "right" side of the tracks has to hide his involvement with hot rods and rock and roll on the "wrong" side of the tracks from his family. The kid, John Ashley, eventually bands together with Gene Vincent's crazed hot rod gang as they gather money for a big drag race.

For *Hot Rod Gang*, George Barris leased from the studios the Richard Peters' 1929 Ford pickup *Ala Kart*, which he had built and shown, along with a 1932 roadster. Barris maintained both of these eye-catching hot rods and oversaw their use on the set.

George (right) on the set with a cream '32 roadster making sure it was treated properly. He also dealt with any mechanical requirements or special filming needs when the car was used. In the scene about to be shot, the rod will follow the camera truck down the road in a high-speed police chase.

106

The poster for *Hot Rod Gang* featured the Barris show-winning hot rod *Ala* Kart, even though it only appeared in the film for a brief time. This lineup of roadsters from one of the street scenes is right out of the fifties with whitewalls and channeled highboys. George helped to coordinate the use of these rods in the movie.

This scene, from the set of *Hot Rod Gang*, shows one of Hollywood's most famous camera cars on the left. This custom-bodied Chrysler Windsor camera platform was used for many years; it allowed cameramen to mount their cameras in many different positions for both high and low angle shots. In this scene, two hot rods follow the camera car down a twisty country highway.

Mag Wheels

Action/comedy/romance movie in 1979; George Barris, Irwin Shaffer, and Colleen Meeker, producers; George Barris, director. Starred: Phoebe Schmidt, Steven Rose, John McLaughlin, and George, Shirley, Brett, and JoJi Barris.

Action/comedy/romance movie in 1979; George Barris, Irwin Shaffer, and Colleen Meeker, producers; George Barris, director. Starred: Phoebe Schmidt, Steven Rose, John McLaughlin, Shelly Horner, Fred Schmidt, and Berkina Flower, with special appearances by George Barris, Shirley Barris, Brett Barris, and JoJi Barris.

This street-action movie centered around van and truck cruising and was set in the future. As World War III raged on, the entire Barris family appeared in this feature with George Barris playing The King of Kustoms (what else?). Meanwhile, son Brett performed stunts while wife Shirley played a housewife. Daughter JoJi got in on the action as well, riding a motorcycle into a lake.

A scene in *Mag Wheels* was set at the Barris shop in North Hollywood. The back area was turned into a van conversion company called Mother Trucker just for the movie. George played himself in the film and also built half a dozen special vans for the scenes; at times he was the director. That's George in the center in the white T-shirt.

Mag Wheels was filmed in the mid-1970s when vans and trucks were just becoming popular. The story line partly revolves around girls who own high-performance trucks and boys who own high-performance vans. The camera crew is about to film a hill climbing competition between them. As you can see, there is a mass of Dodge, Ford, and Chevy trucks lined up for the scene.

VAN & TRUCKIN' MOVIE

STARRING

JOHN McLAUGHLIN   SHELLEY HORNER   BERKINA FLOWER

PHOEBE SCHMIDT   STEVEN ROSE   FRED SCHMIDT

Special Appearance by GEORGE BARRIS

Music Written by   Music Performed by
BILL SCHERECK   "THE WORD"

Produced by   Written and Directed by
COLLEEN MEEKER   BETHEL BUCKALEW

Executive Producers GEORGE BARRIS and IRWIN SCHAEFFER

R RESTRICTED   A PETER PERRY PICTURES RELEASE

The promotional poster for *Mag Wheels*.

Pit Stop

Documentary television movie in 1967 (black and white); Jack Hill, producer. Starred: Brian Donlevy, George Barris, Harry Schooler, with music by the Daily Flash.

Pit Stop was a television documentary originally titled *The Winner*. Basically, it was a dramatized documentary created to profile automotive sports and the different types of individuals involved in them. In the film, custom car king George Barris appeared as himself, playing an automotive designer working for the owner of an outfit called California Custom Cars.

The show featured numerous high-speed scenes, including figure eight racing at Ascot, oval track racing at Whiteman Stadium, and dune buggy competitions. Vintage wrecking yard scenes taken at the old Wilshire Auto Wrecking Yard in Los Angeles, California, added a great feeling of nostalgia. The Barris Kustom shop was

The *Mystique,* a chopped-top full-sized 1965 Buick hardtop that featured a 2½in chop, a custom tubular grille, and matching rear end treatment, is seen here being filmed for *Pit Stop* behind the Buick *Villa Riviera.* The Buick's radical W-shaped front end treatment used French Cibie headlights hidden behind the chromed three-tube grille. There were massive sheet metal changes to the front and rear end of the Buick along with a fully shaved body, molded drip rail, and no quarter windows. The Buick's wild custom bodywork created a mass of interest when it was done in late 1965. It appeared on many magazine covers including the January 1965 cover of *Popular Customs,* an Argus publication. The Buick was finished in apricot pearl with tangerine pearl panels on the hood and fenders. The Buick also appeared in a seventies TV gangster movie called *Run, Buddy, Run.*

even used as setting for part of the movie. Barris did a great job, showing off his automobiles as well as his talent as an actor.

Pit Stop used many Barris machines, including The Mystique, a Buick Wildcat custom, a custom Excalibur sports car, Alvin's Safety Car (which was still under construction), and the Calico Surfer hot rod. This rare movie is now available on home video.

In this scene from Pit Stop, shot in one of the workshops at Barris Kustom Industries, actors and crew mill around the half-completed Alvin's Safety Car as Brian Donlevy reviews his script seated in the chair. Note the original plastic roof bubbles from the building of the Batmobile are still hanging from the roof.

Here George and Donlevy rehearse a section of the movie before filming starts. Note the movie camera mounted on the wheeled dolly which moved along beside the car as the actors went through their lines for this scene. The two are seated in the Calico Surfer, a futuristic woody wagon George had just finished for a customer. Most of the wood body was stained in a pale blue tint which blended with the body color. The Calico Surfer was Mustang GT powered with a hopped-up 289 V-8, custom tube frame and IRS front suspension.

Race with Destiny

Movie biography in 1995; Mardi Rustam, director; Cheeni Productions. Starred: Casper Van Dien, Robert Mitchum, Carrie Mitchum, Diane Ladd, Connie Stevens, Joseph Campanella, Casey Kasem, and Mike Connors.

Race with Destiny was a movie based on fact. It portrayed the story of the ill-fated love affair between James Dean and actress Pier Angeli. It was shot on location where James Dean lived and loved until his death at the wheel of his Porsche 550 Spyder outside Chalome, California.

Coincidentally, Barris had become acquainted with James Dean in the early 1950s when Dean visited his shop (driving the Porsche in which he was later killed). For this dramatization of Dean, Barris built the cars for the film and oversaw all of the stunts involving the vehicles.

For *Race with Destiny*, George built a replica silver Porsche 550 Spyder. Powered by a flat-four VW engine, the replica had a heavily reinforced floor and a heavy-duty powertrain to cope with the rigors of the action scenes. The doors were molded closed to further strengthen the body. This scene shows Casper Van Dien seated on the engine in a white T-shirt being made up for a scene.

For the crash scene the Porsche was mounted on a set of rollers under the driver's-side wheels. This allowed the film crew to rig the car so that it would spin out as they jerked it sideways with a set of hidden cables attached to the truck in the background. This scene was shot several times from different angles and eventually cut together in the editing room to recreate the crash.

Thunder Alley

Romance/action movie in 1967; Burt Topper, producer; Richard Rush, director; American International Pictures. Starred: Annette Funicello, Fabian, Jan Murray, Warren Berlinger, Maureen Arthur, and Diane McBain.

*T*hunder Alley was another teenage formula movie of the mid-sixties. Featuring the usual suspects and juvenile delinquents, it was packed with fast cars, pretty girls, and nights on the beach. The poster for the movie summed it all up in one line: "Days of Screaming Wheels—Nights of Reckless Pleasure."

Teen idol Fabian played a stock car driver who keeps blacking out at the wheel of his race car. This gets him suspended from racing, but he still gets to chase after the girls when he recovers. There is plenty of action, music, and passion in *Thunder Alley* as Fabian races by in the face of death and chases girls with lustful abandon. It was another tall order for the versatile Barris.

For the film, he was asked to create a special *Thunder Charger* based on a production 1967 Dodge Charger. Just as he did with the Buick Riviera in 1964, Barris hit the drawing board and sketched out a Targa coupe, featuring a can-

The Dodge was designed on paper then, using a 1967 Hemi-powered Charger fastback, George modified it with a futuristic "concept car" look including matching front and rear tunnels. However, the bodywork retained both factory taillights and a stock Dodge grille from another Dodge. He opened up the roof, as he had on the *Villa Riviera* several years earlier, but this time with a deeper cantilever.

There were four major sections of work to be done to create the *Thunder Charger*. Here George supervises the finishing of the cantilevered roof with bodyman Carl Cooley. Note the shaved door handles.

Dodge supplied him with a new Charger for the project. George is seen here in front of his workshop in North Hollywood looking over the plans just after the car arrived.

tilevered roof with a removable Targa roof section that stored in the trunk. This section could easily be latched into place, turning the Targa back into a coupe.

A shopping list of modifications followed: first, the rear was extended along the front. A new spoiler was built into the rear deck. To help create an energetic, custom look, a new set of taillights and a redesigned grille were added. The grille was made with four French Cibie headlights set back into a stock Dodge grille. The front bumper was removed and both fenders extended 8in forward into blade-like tips. A completely new rolled pan formed the lower part of the grille opening.

The hood was set with slanted hood scoops that gave a racy edge to the new front end. These scoops, noted by Dodge stylists, were

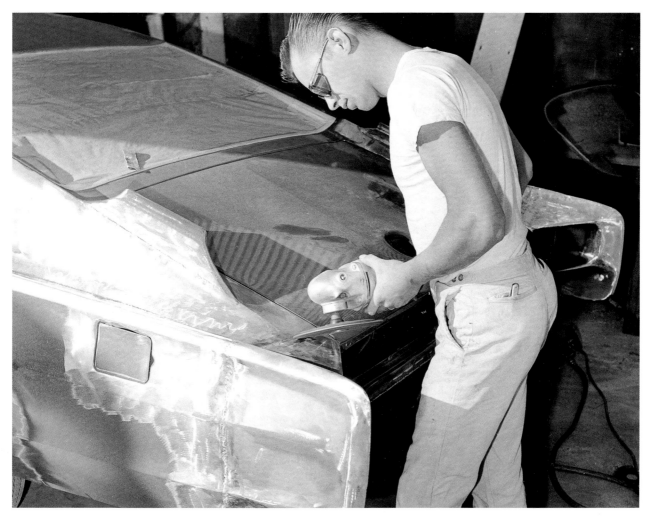

The tips of the rear fenders were extended 6in after the rear bumper was removed and replaced with a new rolled rear pan. The mounts for the rear wing can be seen above the gas door as the bodyman finishes off the welding on the fender extension supporting the new tunneled rear end.

immediately picked up as a new design element. Evidently, leading industry designers liked the idea since the Barris-style scoops later appeared in several Chrysler production models, including the GTX, Barracuda, Challenger, and Charger.

To match the line of the new front fenders, the rear fenders were extended 6in. This created enough space for the body men to fabricate a tunneled rear section for the full-width, stock Charger taillight. Now it was seated deep inside of the new rear bodywork. Functional side panel scoops were also grafted onto the rear quarter panels with their ducting pushing air into the rear brakes. To finish it off, an adjustable rear deck spoiler was built across the trunk lid.

Powering this beautiful *Thunder Charger* was a stock, factory 427 Hemi V-8 that delivered its raw horsepower via a Chrysler 727 Torqueflite

Annette Funicello gets ready for another take. From this angle you can see how the roof was notched to further open up the passenger compartment and give a detailed sense of style to the roof conversion.

The car attracted a lot of attention with its new body graphics. The yellow and black center panels were very wild for the time and the reworked front fenders, in red and yellow and blue-toned feather graphics on the rear, certainly gave the *Thunder Charger* a new look.

automatic transmission. The body was painted in twenty coats of acrylic lacquer using gold Murano pearl, layered over with ten coats of Metalflake white, along with some decorative side panel fade-aways in candy apple red and purple.

After the movie was completed, a new set of wild, psychedelic graphics in yellow and black

were added, along with striking blue and purple rear quarter panel feather graphics. Not afraid to strut its stuff in public, the Barris *Thunder Charger* went on an extensive national publicity tour shortly after *Thunder Alley* was released. Later, the model maker MPC issued a one-twenty-fifth scale model kit of this dreamy Dodge custom.

The *Thunder Charger* went on a national promotional tour immediately after the movie was released. It was repainted with these wild graphics and appeared outside movie theaters, at drag strips, in shopping malls, and at car shows around the country. MPC released a one-twenty-fifth scale model of the car, which today is rare and highly collectable.

Chapter Seven

Specialty Vehicles

The Beach Boys' Mini Surfer

Specialty Music Car for Capitol Records

During the late sixties, truth was often stranger than fiction. One of the most prominent examples of this axiom was the amazing success of the rock-and-roll group, the Beach Boys. Without ever really touching a surf board, they managed to create a lasting image of Southern California: blond-headed beach boys who dream only of waves, cars, and girls.

Fanciful as it was, the idealized craze to "catch a wave" rolled across the country, resulting in a number of hit records for the group. As more and more teenagers were thrilling to the good vibrations, Capitol Records decided it was time to capitalize on the Beach Boys' surfing songs with a custom surf car.

The Beach Boys appeared at the Barris shop in North Hollywood for this promotional picture before any of the give-away Mokes made it out to the radio stations. Al Jardine is on the roof and the rest of the group is seated left to right: Brian Wilson, Dennis Wilson, Mike Love, and Carl Wilson.

Candy stripes went in every direction. The seats were covered with bright red and white fur fabric while the roof was trimmed in stripes with a fringe around the edge, and the body was cross-striped to match. Gold records were used as wheel covers on the first five and were given to the Beach Boys for their personal use.

In early 1966, Barris was asked to build a series of modified Austin Mini Mokes to be dubbed the *Mini Surfers*. The plan was for the cars to be built in two groups. The first five were designed for the Beach Boys themselves and featured candy-stripe paint treatments, matching striped tops, and wheels with gold record hubcaps. A Dewey

Weber surfboard was attached to each roof.

Later that year, the second series of twenty *Mini Surfer* Mokes were constructed. These promo vehicles were used as give-away cars for the radio stations that produced exclusive Capitol Records promotions for the album *The Greatest Hits of the Beach Boys*.

Elvis Presley's Limo

1960 Cadillac Fleetwood Kustom Limousine Specialty music industry car.

The custom Elvis Cadillac Limousine was a classic vehicle in its day, an opulent expression of how successful Elvis was and the extremes that designers would go to to satisfy the excesses of American automania. Unfortunately, Elvis didn't get to use the one-of-a-kind limo as much as he would have liked. During its heyday, it used up most of its early mileage touring the world.

There was good reason for the excitement. The body was painted with custom gold murano pearl with portholes cut into the roof pillars on each side. Real gold plating was used for highlighting on the Eldorado Brougham hubcaps in addition to jazzing up much of the interior trim.

Unlike ordinary Cadillac limos, Barris' tribute to conspicuous consumption (and the recording industry) sported a circular rear lounge complete with a full-buttoned interior and a headliner that featured a set of replica gold records. With a movable partition, the rear compartment had the ability to be screened off from the driver. Other features of the private seating area included a record storage draw, cocktail bar, gold-plated television, radio, record player, refrigerated ice chest, and a vanity dresser.

The interior of the Elvis Cadillac had everything imaginable in automotive comfort. On the left is a record player, in the center the drinks cooler, and to the right is a full sound system for radio, TV, or records. A gold-plated black-and-white TV sat on top of the cabinet in the front of the rear compartment between the bar on the left and the vanity cabinet on the right. Note the gold records on the roof.

This rare photo of Elvis with the 1960 Fleetwood Cadillac was shot at a car show in Hollywood. It was unusual for Elvis to appear in public with his cars like this and it was one of the few times he got to see his Cadillac before it went off on a worldwide tour. George had just finished customizing the car with a new interior, and a wild coat of gold murano pearl paint. The rear compartment could be screened off for privacy and the portholes featured monogrammed E.P. curtains.

■

"Three cheers for George Barris!
Now I see why the young man who
fashioned the now-legendary
Partridge bus for us has himself
become a Hollywood legend.
His body of work is awesome."
Shirley Jones

Paul Revere and the Raiders' Coach

Specialty music industry promotional vehicle; toy licensing vehicle.

The *Raiders' Coach* was a wild idea that George Barris proposed to Paul Revere and Mark Lindsay, leaders of Paul Revere and the Raiders. Barris had already customized a Rolls-Royce and an Excalibur for Lindsay and had done work on Revere's Ferrari. The group asked the Kustom man to come up with a promotional car that would bring more attention to the band.

At his drawing board, Barris penciled out a concept for the *Raiders' Coach*, blending his ideas of an eighteenth century coach with the wildest Detroit high-performance specs he could find. It was decided that horsepower would come from a pair of Pontiac GTO engines to be configured as a four wheeled tractor unit that would pull the powerless coach. The trailing coach and the tractor would be articulated in the middle so that coach and motor would turn like a typical eighteen wheeler with reefer. It was a never before attempted idea that captivated the group and Barris was commissioned to start work.

First, he obtained a pair of 428 Pontiac engines and the front clip from a 1968 GTO and decked them out with Moon and Pontiac performance parts, chrome, and custom-made accessories. The chassis for the tractor unit was built with a center backbone and a tube front axle with a center-mounted shock absorber. This allowed Barris to hang the engines on the outside of the frame for maximum effect. The engines were coupled through a chain-drive arrangement at the tail of the automatic transmissions and could be run together or independently. Power was transferred from this drive system to a reverse center axle on the middle wheel set. A pair of radiators with electric fans were mounted over the transmissions to run the cooling system.

The front suspension employed torsion bars while the other axles were mounted using custom-made, chromed leaf springs that were also designed to form part of the coach's detailing. Barris had the coach body built out of steel and oak hardwood to give the look and feel of a true stagecoach. It was trimmed with wicker cane side panels and painted in black and yellow with a matching yellow square tufted interior and curtains.

The trailer unit for the *Coach* had a control panel complete with steering, instruments, and a gear selector mounted up front—just like a traditional coach. Since the unconventional steering was mounted on the coach rather than tractor, it was controlled with hydraulics. The system was a Barris innovation using an aircraft control system, hydraulic rams, pumps, and hoses.

Like the *Voxmobile* Barris would build later, the *Raiders' Coach* featured a hefty installation of

George designed the *Raiders Coach* to be as wild and as wacky as possible for Paul Revere and the Raiders. It featured a unique drive system that coupled two Pontiac engines to drive a single center axle. Like a tractor/trailer unit, the *Coach* featured three axles and a midmounted driving station positioned like a traditional stagecoach.

The GTO front clip on the *Raiders' Coach* was painted in GTO judge carousel red. A set of antique headlights were installed along with a matching set of running and taillights. New engine side covers were fashioned from a set of Vox speakers, and a pair of padded seats were installed on the roof to provide comfortable seating space for the group during parades and performances. The *Raiders' Coach* was quite a piece of engineering. Its innovative ideas were far more complex than many of the cars George had previously built.

The steel-framed backbone chassis was bent and welded up from U and box section tubing. The *Coach's* suspension was also very innovative yet reminiscent of what stage coaches had used during the last century, with leaf springs mounted solidly at one end and an axle riding on the other end of the spring. The dual 428ci Pontiac engines were slung off the center backbone chassis on the tractor unit with dual fan-cooled radiators mounted over the transmissions.

The group posed with George and the coach for this publicity shot high above Los Angeles, dressed in their colonial Raiders outfits. The huge Vox drum set can be seen inside the coach along with the mandatory Vox guitars. The *Coach* rolled on a set of custom-made Cragar wheels, which were capped with Firestone Super Sport tires on the truck unit and 18in heavy truck tires on the rear.

Vox music equipment. He fitted a double Vox Super Continental keyboard complete with amplifiers and speakers, a full Vox drum set, and three Vox Beatle amplifiers that could power up to twelve electric guitars. For the crowning touch, six Vox electric guitars were slung in saddlebags off the side of the *Coach*.

At the time, the bill for the *Raiders' Coach* was $85,000. That's $300,000 in today's money! But it was money well spent. The *Coach* traveled the country appearing at concerts and car shows where promoters found it was the number one attraction. MPC, the model kit maker, hastily introduced a plastic assembly kit for the *Raiders' Coach*. Snapped up by eager fans of Paul Revere and the Raiders, it became one of their top selling kits that year.

George used a pair of 428 Pontiac engines which he decorated with Moon and Pontiac performance parts. These engines hung off a center backbone that formed the chassis for the tractor unit which was built with a tube axle and a center-mounted shock absorber. This allowed the engines to hang on the outside of the frame for maximum visual effect. The engines could be run together or independently and were coupled, through a chain-drive arrangement at the tail, to automatic transmissions.

The Voxmobile

Specialty music industry promotional vehicle. Built for the Vox Guitar Division of the Thomas Organ Company.

VOX KART   VOX

GEO. BARRIS
BARRIS KUSTOM CITY 3·1·67

When promotional director T. Warren Hampton of the Vox Guitar company approached George Barris, he came with a $30,000 budget and a desire to have an unprecedented type of vehicle built. First and foremost, it had to look just like a guitar. Second, it had to be completely driveable and fully functional as a working vehicle. What's more, it would be a two-seat roadster that would incorporate a huge, fully operational Vox organ and amplifier. Undaunted by the request, Barris put together a series of proposals and then met with Joseph Benaron, president of Vox Guitars. He pitched a roadster design that used a pair of guitars in profile for the sides and a huge, built-in Vox amplifier in the trunk. That way, the *Voxmobile* could be used as a completely portable, and highly visible, Vox products demonstrator.

Initially, the design was styled as a guitar with electronic accessories. This remained basic to the design as Barris further refined the roadster by incorporating other Vox products into the machine. To achieve this, he fashioned the grille from the same cross rib pattern as the speaker covers used on Vox amps.

The *Voxmobile* was powered with a Cobra-packaged 289 Ford V-8, and a Ford automatic transmission. The engine was dressed up and fitted with an oversized cooling system to prevent overheating in parades. Its one-of-a-kind air cleaner was rigged with a guitar-shaped neck and topped off with a Vox speaker horn.

On the inside and the outside, Barris Kustoms pushed this creation to the extreme. First, a full tube frame was fabricated. The body was formed of steel tubing and wood, and was covered with a mixture of fiberglass and plastic. Then, the silhouette of two giant guitars were incorporated, complete with frets, strings, and

Originally proposed as the *Vox Kart*, these design illustrations show how little the concept changed when the *Voxmobile* roadster rolled out of the Barris shop. Designed in 1967 and built in 1968, the *Voxmobile* featured a custom double tube space frame and was powered by a Hi-Po packaged Ford 289 Cobra V-8, C-4 automatic and a Ford 9in rear axle.

tuning keys. A pair of Vox Guitars were mounted like tail fins at the rear. Barris even built in chromed running boards so that three guitarists and a keyboard player had a place to stand and play when the *Voxmobile* appeared in parades. Inside, it was custom trim all the way with

The *Voxmobile* appeared on the TV show *Groovy* with host Mike Blodgett and the band Strawberry Alarm Clock. The show was filmed on Venice Beach and featured a crowd of hundreds who watched, danced, and went wild on the beach as part of the show. It also appeared on the TV quiz show *Dialing for Dollars*. The *Voxmobile* was also used in trade show displays and even received some exposure at some hot rod and auto show events around the country.

wrap-around windscreen, Masland Duran black vinyl, and Mouton Fur carpeting. Outside, a combo of thirty coats of metalflake fire red with white pearl fought for attention with the gleaming chrome of the Rader wheels.

Completely self-contained, this rolling soundstage featured three Vox Beatle amplifiers and a twelve-speaker installation of bass, mid-range, and tweeters. Barris styled the bodywork in order to make room for a master electronics control that allowed thirty-two electric guitars to be plugged into jacks, all mounted along the top edge of the bodywork! A Vox Continental organ was mounted in the trunk area as well. For backup sound, a Muntz Stereo Tape Cartridge system was also installed

so that music could be played when there were no live musicians available.

This unique, portable electronics package was powered by a pair of 450-watt inverters, pulling amperage from the engine alternator and twelve-volt battery. It was a clever layout that permitted the *Voxmobile* to be used as a concert attraction or be played at shows and promotional demonstrations. Many artists took advantage of the *Voxmobile's* features, including Jimmy Bryant, "The World's Fastest Guitarist." Under promotional contract to use Vox products when the roadster was initially built, he later appeared in a series of Vox print advertisements and even featured the rolling guitar machine on one of his record albums.

The Voxmobile appeared in many Vox advertisements with Jimmy Bryant, renowned as "The World's Fastest Guitarist." Jimmy is seen here with the Ford Cobra 289 V-8-powered *Voxmobile* before a photo session for a Vox. The roadster featured a hot rod-style chassis with a chromed drop tube axle up front and a regular coil spring rear suspension. On the road, the *Voxmobile* had plenty of punch from the Cobra V-8, as the entire car weighed under 2,000lb.

Index

A Boy, A Girl, 14, 15
Alvin the Chipmunk and Friends, 15
American Sunroof Corporation, 38
AMT Corporation, 96, 100

Barris, Sam, 8, 9, 82
Barris kustom cars:
    Ala Kart, 8, 106, 107
    Alvin's Safety Car, 15, 111
    Batcycle, 26
    Batmobile, 10
    Batmobile, 13, 16, 20-26
    Big Bear Scrambler, 99
    Car, 17, 28-32
    De Elegance, 50
    Drag-u-la, 13, 68-71, 73
    Fuzz Car, 102
    Groovy Ocelot, 97
    Hirohata Mercury, 8
    KITT (Knight Industries Two-Thousand), 42-45
    Lethal Weapon, 57
    Mannix Roadster, 47, 48
    Manta, 40
    Mini Surfer, 118, 119
    Mongrel T, 92, 93
    Munster Koach, 12, 13, 66-71, 73
    Petty's #43 NASCAR racer (replica), 36, 38
    Presley Limousine, 120, 121
    Raiders' Coach, 14, 122-124
    Super Styling Experimental Roadster (SSXR), 34-39
    Surf Woody, 14
    The Calico Surfer, 15, 111
    The Mystique, 111
    Thunder Charger, 113-117
    Villa Riviera, 76-81, 110
    Voxmobile, 17, 18, 125-127
    XMSC-210, 11
    Zebra Mustang, 14, 84, 85
    ZZR, 15, 98, 100
Batman, 12, 20-27
Beach Boys, 118, 119
Blystone, John, 7
Burn 'em Up Barnes, 7

Conway, Hershel "Junior", 8
Cooley, Carl, 34, 114
Creach, Everett, 28

Daktari, 14
Darro, Frankie, 7
Dean, Dick, 58, 73
Dean, Keith, 73
Dick Tracy, 19, 33

Easy Come, Easy Go, 92, 93
Ertl, 40

Fireball 500, 14, 34
For Those Who Think Young, 12, 76-81

Geraghty, John, 65
Good Times, 15, 94-96
Groovy, 17, 97, 127

Hardcastle and McCormick, 40
Henning, Paul, 11
Here Comes the Munsters, 73

High School Confidential, 882, 83
Hot Car Girl (Hot Rod Girl), 8
Hot Rod Gang, 8, 9, 106, 107
Hot Rod Girl, 8
Hot Rod Rumble, 8

It Started with a Kiss, 20, 25

Jurassic Park, 41

Keystone Cops, 7
Knight Rider, 42-45
Korkes, Richard, 26, 84
Kunz, Bud, 25, 50, 70

Lincoln Futura, 20, 25

Mag Wheels, 108, 109
Mannix, 15, 46-69
Marriage on the Rocks, 14, 84-87
Martinson, Leslie, 76, 77
Model Products Company (MPC), 48, 63, 90, 97, 116, 124
Munster, Go Home, 72
Munsters Today, 73
My Lips Betray, 7
My Mother the Car, 14, 14

North by Northwest, 8, 10

Oldfield, Barney, 7
Out of Sight, 15, 98-100

Paul Revere and the Raiders, 14, 122-124
Perry Mason, 78, 81
Pit Stop, 15, 110, 111
Playing Mantis, 100
Presley, Elvis, 120, 121

Race for Life, 7
Race with Destiny, 112
Road Demon, 7
Romp, 15, 101-103
Running Wild, 8

Super Van, 88, 89

The 300 Yard Drive, 7
The Beverly Hillbillies, 12, 54-57
The Bugaloos, 17, 90, 91
The Car, 17, 28-32
The Cool Hot Rod, 8
The Crowd Roars, 7
The Flintstones, 19, 58-61
The Good Guys, 15, 17, 62, 63
The Many Loves of Dobie Gillis, 11, 64, 65
The Munsters, 13, 66-73
The Patsy, 11
The Silencers, 14, 50-53
The Time Machine, 8, 10
The Van, 75
Thunder Alley, 15, 113-117
Tompkins, Les, 25, 50, 70

Village of the Giants, 14, 104, 105
Vox Guitar Company, 17, 125

Window on Main Street, 9, 11